*To be a disciple and missionary of the Lord Jesus
we must know his Word written in the Gospels.*

*With my blessing,
Francis*

GOD WITH US

THE LIFE-CHANGING STORY OF JESUS

Ramon Pane Foundation

NEW CATHOLIC EDITION

www.godwithus.live

English print: 979-8-9852178-0-3
English e-book: 979-8-9852178-5-8
English audio book: 979-8-9852178-6-5

The Ramon Pane Foundation takes its name from one of the greatest
figures in the evangelization of America. It was founded in 1994 in
honor of Ramón Pané, who is considered to be the first missionary
to America. It is an international group of Catholics whose mission is
to help diocese and Catholic organizations in educational, missionary,
and spiritual training.

For more information about FRP's mission and work, visit
www.fundacionpane.org.

CONTENTS

INTRODUCTION

Many people have questions about Jesus. Most people don't know much about him. They might know only what they have heard from others, but some want to find out more. They wonder if what Christians say about him is true. Can he really bring them peace? Can he bring them closer to God?

Jesus Christ was born in a small Jewish village 2,000 years ago. He was a carpenter until he was about 30 years old. Then he became a teacher and healer. He traveled less than 100 miles from his home, and his mission work lasted no more than three years. He preached about God's love and performed many miracles. He attracted a large group of followers. But the religious leaders were afraid of him, so they arrested him and convinced the Roman authorities to crucify him.

Jesus' followers reported that he came back to life and returned to heaven. They believed in Jesus even though many were put in jail or killed for following him. They became known as "Christians" and spread Jesus' message throughout the world.

WHY IS JESUS SO IMPORTANT?

Jesus Christ has affected history more than any other person. What he did changed the world forever. His followers are members of the world's largest religion—there are now more than two billion Christians around the world.

Jesus had a very important message. He talked about God and about life after death. Jesus made some amazing claims about himself. He said, "I haven't come down from heaven to do my own will; I've come to do the will of the one who sent me." John 6:38 He claimed he was the Son of God who was sent because "God loved the world so much that he gave his one and only Son so that anyone who believes in him may not die but have eternal life." John 3:16

Many people have believed in Jesus and found his promises to be true. He has brought faith, hope, and purpose to millions of people. They have come to know Jesus as a real friend, and he changed their lives.

Jesus preached the good news about God's love for everyone. Yet some people did not believe his message. Jesus told them, "The words you hear me saying aren't my own. They belong to the Father who sent me." John 14:24 He warned them, "There is a judge for anyone who doesn't accept me and my words. The words I've spoken will judge them on the last day." John 12:48

HOW DO WE KNOW ABOUT JESUS?

Accounts of Jesus' life were written not long after he died. They are called Gospels (*gospel* means "good news"). These Gospel accounts became part of the Bible that we have today.

Some other Jewish and Roman writers also mention Jesus. Most history scholars today agree that Jesus really did live 2,000 years ago.

There are four Gospel accounts in the Bible: these are the Gospels of Matthew, Mark, Luke, and John. The Gospel accounts came from reports by Jesus' followers and by others who knew him.

Jesus chose 12 of his many followers to travel with him, and he called that small group his disciples. They gave personal reports about the things that Jesus said and did.

Matthew was one of the disciples. Before he met Jesus, he collected taxes for the Romans. Matthew's Gospel was meant for Jewish people. It explains how the Jewish Scriptures revealed who Jesus really is. His Gospel connects the Old and New Testaments of the Bible.

Mark was a young man who followed Jesus. He was not one of the disciples, but he helped Simon Peter, one of the disciples closest to Jesus. The first Christians met in Mark's mother's house for prayer. Mark's Gospel is a short history of the life and message of Jesus. Many Bible scholars think that Mark's Gospel was the earliest of the four—written in about AD 70.

Luke was a doctor who knew the disciples. Luke may have learned from Jesus' mother, Mary, many of the things he wrote. Luke said, "I also have looked into everything very carefully myself, going right back to the beginning. I've decided to write down an orderly account for you." Luke 1:2-3 Luke also wrote the book of Acts, which describes how the Christian church began.

John was another of the disciples who was a fisherman before he met Jesus. Like Matthew, John traveled with Jesus and saw the things that Jesus did. John's Gospel is about who Jesus really is and why he came. It explains that Jesus is God who became a human being to show us what God is like and to die for our sins.

Before the four Gospels were written, the stories about Jesus were handed down by word of mouth. Most people were not able to read at the time of Jesus, so they remembered the sermons of well-known preachers and passed them on. The reports of what Jesus said and what he did were told over and over again.

These reports were included in the Gospels. Luke stated, "Many others have already written about the things that have taken place among us, based on reports passed down from eyewitnesses." Luke 1:1-2 Many of those eyewitnesses were still alive when the Gospels were written.

The Gospels were collected with other writings of the early church. This collection is known as the New Testament of the Bible and is all about the life and message of Jesus Christ.

The Christian church carefully copied and saved the New Testament. We have more copies of the New Testament sources than of any other writings from that time in history.

Jesus and his disciples spoke Aramaic, the language of the Jewish people. But the Gospel writers wrote in Greek, which was a common language of the Roman Empire.

The first English translation of the Greek New Testament was printed in the 1500s. The translation was revised when older copies of the New Testament were found. Bible translations are updated from time to time as scholars study the original sources, and changes in language occur.

There are now many different translations of the Bible. Some are word-for-word translations; others are more like a thought-for-thought translation. Some Bibles use elegant, old-fashioned language; other Bibles use modern, everyday language. The new Catholic Edition of this book uses the *Radiate*™ translation of the New Testament, produced in collaboration with Catholic scholars. It faithfully translates the original meaning of the Gospels into modern English that is easy to read for young people, and people with English as a second language.

WHAT IS THIS BOOK?

God with Us uses verses from the Gospels of Matthew, Mark, Luke, and John woven together into a single story (known as a "blended harmony"). This makes it easy to read a single chronological account of the life and message of Jesus Christ. The format is similar to a biography but uses only Scripture from the Bible. The Bible verses used to tell the story of Jesus are indicated at the end of each selection.

None of the four Gospels alone give a complete picture of Jesus' life, because each Gospel writer chose to highlight different things. The details and order of the events are sometimes different. The purpose of the story was more important than the details of how, where, and when they happened.

The Gospel writers sometimes wrote about similar things happening at a different time or place. Scholars do not always agree on whether these were different events or not. It is likely that Jesus preached the same message on more than one occasion.

Putting this story together required many decisions. Sometimes, when details in the Gospels differ, the text found in more than one Gospel was chosen. Otherwise, the Gospel was selected that best helps you follow the story.

The study resources provided at the end of the book include a list of Bible references and an index for events in the life of Jesus. You can use this list to find and compare each of the Gospel accounts. There is also a guide to the people and terms in the story for readers who are new to the Bible. The study resources give personal reflections for each chapter, based on the ancient method of *Lectio Divina*, and discussion questions for you to go deeper into the message of Jesus.

This book is by no means intended to replace the Bible. It was written to bring the good news of what Jesus said and did to people who otherwise might not know it. We hope you will read the message of Jesus, understand it, and be inspired to follow the teaching and example of Jesus in your life.

CHAPTER 1

GOD REACHES OUT

In the beginning was the Word, and the Word was with God, and the Word was God. He was with God in the beginning. All things were made through him; nothing that has been made was made without him. In him was life, and that life was the light for all people. The light shines in the darkness, and the darkness has not overcome it.

The true light that gives light to everyone was coming into the world. He was in the world, and the world was made through him, but the world did not recognize him. He came to what was his own, but his own people didn't accept him. But to everyone who did accept him and believed in his name, he gave the right to become children of God, not children born to human parents, or because of human choice or a husband's wishes, but born of God.

The Word became human and made his home with us. We have seen his glory, the glory of the One and Only, who came from the Father, full of grace and truth.

Out of his fullness we have all received grace in place of the grace already given. The law was given through Moses, but grace and truth came through Jesus Christ.

No one has ever seen God. But the One and Only, who is God and who is at the Father's side, has made him known. John 1:1-5, 9-14, 16-18

Just as many others have already written about the things that have taken place among us, based on reports passed down from eyewitnesses, I [Luke] also have looked into everything very carefully myself, going right back to the beginning. I've decided to write down an orderly account for you, most excellent Theophilus, because I want you to know that what you've been taught is true.

During the time when Herod was king of Judea, there was a priest named Zechariah. He belonged to the group of priests named after Abijah. His wife was named Elizabeth, and she also came from the line of priests descended from Aaron. Both of them did what was right in God's sight; they obeyed all of the Lord's commands and instructions faithfully. But they didn't have children, because Elizabeth was infertile, and by that point they were both very old.

One day Zechariah's group was on duty, and he was serving as a priest in God's temple. He had been chosen by lot (which was how the priests were assigned duties) to go into the temple of the Lord, where he was supposed to burn incense. When the time came for him to do this, all the people who had gathered to worship were praying outside.

Just then an angel of the Lord appeared to Zechariah. The angel came and stood at the right side of the incense altar. When Zechariah saw him, he was amazed and terrified. But the angel said to him, "Don't be afraid, Zechariah, your prayer has been heard—your wife Elizabeth is going to have a baby boy! You must name him John. He will be a joy and a delight to you, and his birth will also make many other people glad, because he will become such a great man in Lord's sight. He must never drink wine or other alcohol. He will be filled with the Holy Spirit before he is even born. He will bring many of the people of Israel back to the Lord their God. Having the same spirit and power as Elijah, he will go ahead of the Lord, creating peace between parents and their children and teaching people who are disobeying to be wise and do what is right. In this way, he will make sure that the people are ready for the Lord."

Zechariah asked the angel, "How can I know that this will happen? I'm an old man, and my wife is old too."

The angel said to him, "I am Gabriel! I'm the angel who stands right next to God! I've been sent to speak to you and tell you this good news. But now you won't be able to speak; you'll have to be silent until after John is born, because you didn't believe my words. They will come true at the time God has chosen."

While all this was happening, the people were waiting for Zechariah to come out of the temple. They were wondering why he was staying in there for so long. When he did come out, he couldn't speak to them. But eventually they understood that he'd seen a vision in the temple because he explained this to them in gestures, even though he didn't get his voice back.

When his time of service was over, he returned home. After that, his wife Elizabeth became pregnant, but she stayed out of sight for five months. "The Lord has done this for me," she said. "In these days, he has been good to me and taken away my shame among the people."

In the sixth month of Elizabeth's pregnancy, God sent the angel Gabriel to Nazareth, a town in Galilee. He was sent to a virgin who was engaged to a man named Joseph, who came from the family line of David. The virgin's name was Mary. The angel went to her and said, "Greetings, favored one! The Lord is with you."

Mary was troubled by these words; she wondered why the angel had greeted her that way. But he said to her, "Don't be afraid, Mary. God has chosen to do something wonderful through you. You're going to become pregnant and give birth to a son, and you will call him Jesus. He will be great, and he will be called the Son of the Most High God. The Lord God will make him a king like his ancestor David, and he will rule over his people, the descendants of Jacob, forever—his kingdom will never end."

"How will this be," Mary asked the angel, "since I'm a virgin?"

The angel answered, "The Holy Spirit will come upon you and the power of the Most High God will overshadow you, so that the holy one who is born will be called the Son of God. Your relative Elizabeth is about to have a child even though she is old. People thought she couldn't have children, but she has been pregnant now for six months. What God says always comes true."

"I am the Lord's servant," Mary answered. "May it happen to me just as you have said." Then the angel left her.

Right away Mary packed up and hurried to the town in Judea's hill country where Zechariah and Elizabeth lived. When she got to their house, she went inside and greeted Elizabeth. As soon as Elizabeth heard Mary's greeting, her baby jumped inside her. Elizabeth was filled with the Holy Spirit and called out in a loud voice, "Blessed are you among all women, and blessed is the child in your womb! But why has God shown me so much favor that the mother of my Lord has come to see me? As soon as I heard the sound of your voice, the baby inside me jumped for joy. Blessed are you, because you believed the Lord would keep his promises to you!"

Mary said,

"My soul cries out that the Lord is great, and my spirit delights in God my Savior.

He has taken note of me, even though I am only his humble servant.

From now on all people will call me blessed, because the Mighty One has done great things for me—his name is holy.

He shows mercy to all those who respect him, from parent to child down through the generations.

He has done mighty things with his powerful arm; he has scattered those who are proud in their deepest thoughts.

He has brought down rulers from their thrones, but he has lifted up people who weren't considered important.

He has filled with good things those who were hungry, but he has sent the rich away empty.

He has helped his servant, the people of Israel, remembering to
be merciful as he promised our fathers, to Abraham and his
descendants forever."

Mary stayed with Elizabeth for about three months, and then she
returned home.

When the time came for Elizabeth to have her baby, she gave
birth to a son. Her neighbors and relatives heard how good the Lord
had been to her and they shared her joy.

On the eighth day, they came to have the child circumcised. They
were going to name him Zechariah, like his father, but his mother
spoke up and said, "No! He has to be called John."

"None of your relatives has that name," they protested.

Then they motioned to his father to find out what he wanted to
name the child. He asked for something to write on, and everyone was
amazed when he wrote, "His name is John." All of a sudden Zechariah could speak again, and right away he started praising God. All of
his neighbors were filled with fear and wonder. Throughout Judea's
hill country, people began talking about all these things. Everyone
who heard what had happened wondered about it. Because the Lord
was with John, they asked, "What is this child going to become?"

John's father Zechariah was filled with the Holy Spirit. He
prophesied,

"Praise the Lord, the God of Israel! He has visited his people and
paid to set them free.
He has acted with great power and saved us through the family
line of his servant David, as the holy prophets long ago said
he would.
He has saved us from our enemies and rescued us from all who
hate us.
He has been merciful to our ancestors and remembered his holy
covenant, the promise he made to our father Abraham.

He promised he would save us from our enemies, so we could serve him without fear in holiness and justice, in his presence, as long as we live.

And you, my child, will be called a prophet of the Most High God, because you will go ahead of the Lord to prepare the way for him, to give his people the knowledge of salvation through the forgiveness of their sins.

All this will happen because our God is tender and merciful; his kindness will make the sun rise for us in the sky.

It will shine on those living in darkness and in the shadow of death, and it will guide our feet onto the path of peace."

The child grew up and his spirit became strong. He stayed in the desert until it was time for him to appear publicly to Israel. Luke 1:1-80

CHAPTER 2

A SPECIAL BIRTH

This is how Jesus the Messiah was born. His mother Mary had promised to marry a man named Joseph. But before they lived together, she became pregnant. This happened by the power of the Holy Spirit, but Joseph didn't know that. He thought that Mary hadn't been faithful to him. He wanted to follow the law of Moses and didn't want to put her to shame in public. So he planned to break up with her quietly.

But as Joseph was thinking about this, an angel of the Lord appeared to him in a dream. The angel said, "Joseph, son of David, don't be afraid to take Mary home as your wife. The baby inside her is from the Holy Spirit. She's going to have a son, and you're to give him the name Jesus, because he will save his people from their sins."

All this took place to make what the Lord had said through the prophet Isaiah come true. He'd said, "The virgin is going to have a baby. She will give birth to a son, and he will be called Immanuel." The name Immanuel means "God with us."

When Joseph got up the next morning, he did just what the angel of the Lord had commanded him to do. He took Mary home as his wife, but he didn't sleep with her before she'd given birth to a son. And Joseph gave him the name Jesus. Matt. 1:18-25

Around this time Caesar Augustus made a law that required everyone in the whole Roman world to register for taxation and military service. This was the first time a registration was required, and it happened while Quirinius was governor of Syria. Everyone had to go to their own hometown to register.

Because Joseph was from the family line of David, he went from Nazareth in Galilee to Judea so he could register there in Bethlehem, the town of David. He went with Mary, who was engaged to him and who was expecting a child. While they were there, the time came for the baby to be born. Mary gave birth to her first child, a boy, and wrapped him in wide strips of cloth. She had to place him in a manger because there was no guest room available for them to stay in.

There were shepherds out in the fields nearby, taking care of their sheep that night. An angel of the Lord appeared to them, and the glory of the Lord shone around them. They were terrified, but the angel said to them, "Don't be afraid! I've brought you good news that will give great joy to all people. Today in the town of David a Savior has been born for you! He is the Messiah, the Lord. Here is how you can recognize him: You'll find a baby wrapped in strips of cloth and lying in a manger."

Suddenly a large group of angels from heaven appeared with the first one, praising God and saying, "Glory to God in the highest heaven! Peace on earth to all those he wants to bless!"

The angels left and went back to heaven. Then the shepherds said to one another, "Let's go to Bethlehem and see this thing that has happened, which the Lord has told us about."

So they hurried off and found Mary and Joseph and the baby, who was lying in the manger. When the shepherds saw him, they told everyone what the angel had said about this child. All who heard it were amazed at what the shepherds said to them. But Mary kept all these things in mind and thought deeply about them.

The shepherds returned, giving glory and praise to God, because everything they'd seen and heard was just as they'd been told.

When the child was eight days old, he was circumcised. Then they named him Jesus, which was the name the angel had given him before his mother became pregnant.

The time came for the purification rituals required by the Law of Moses. So Joseph and Mary took Jesus to Jerusalem, and there they presented him to the Lord. They did this to obey the Law of the Lord, which says, "The first boy born in every family must be set apart for the Lord." They also offered a sacrifice as described in the Law, "a pair of doves or two young pigeons."

A good and godly man named Simeon lived there in Jerusalem. He was waiting for God's promise to Israel to come true, and the Holy Spirit was with him. The Spirit had shown Simeon that he would not die until he had seen the Lord's Messiah.

Prompted by the Spirit, he went into the temple courtyard, and he was there when Jesus' parents brought him in to do for him what the Law required. Simeon took Jesus in his arms and praised God, saying, "Lord, King over all, you have kept your promise and you may now let me, your servant, go in peace, because I have seen your salvation with my own eyes. You have prepared it in the sight of all nations as a light to shine on the Gentiles and as glory for your people Israel."

The child's father and mother were amazed at what was said about him. Then Simeon blessed them. He said to Mary, Jesus' mother, "God has sent this child to cause many people in Israel to fall and to rise. Many will speak against him, and the thoughts of many hearts will be made known. A sword will wound your own soul as well."

A prophet named Anna was also there. She was the daughter of Penuel, who came from the tribe of Asher. Anna was very old. After getting married, she had lived with her husband for seven years, and after he died she had lived as a widow until she was 84. She never left the temple but worshiped night and day, praying and going without food. Anna came up to Jesus' family at that moment. She gave thanks to God and spoke about the child to all who were looking forward to the time when Jerusalem would be set free. Luke 2:1-38

Jesus was born in Bethlehem in Judea while Herod was king. Wise men then came from the east to Jerusalem and asked, "Where is the child who has been born as the new king of the Jews? We saw his star when it rose, and now we've come to worship him."

When King Herod heard about this, he became very concerned, as did everyone else in Jerusalem. He called together all the Jewish chief priests and teachers of the law to ask them where the Messiah was going to be born. "In Bethlehem in Judea," they replied, "because this is what the prophet has written: 'But you, Bethlehem, in the land of Judah, are certainly not the least important of the rulers in Judah. A ruler will come out of you who will care for my people Israel like a shepherd.'"

Then Herod spoke privately with the wise men and found out exactly when the star had appeared. He sent them to Bethlehem and told them, "Go and search carefully for the child. As soon as you find him, send word to me so I can come and worship him too."

After the king had given them these orders, the wise men went on their way. The star they'd seen when it rose went ahead of them and stopped over the place where the child was. When they saw the star, they were filled with joy. The wise men went into the house, and there they saw the child with his mother Mary. They bowed down and worshiped him, and then they opened their treasure chests and gave him gold, frankincense, and myrrh. But because they were warned in a dream not to go back to Herod, they returned to their country by a different way.

After the wise men had left, an angel of the Lord appeared to Joseph in a dream. "Get up!" the angel said. "Take the child and his mother and escape to Egypt! Stay there until I tell you to come back, because Herod is going to try to find the child and kill him."

So Joseph got up in the night and left for Egypt with the child and his mother. They all stayed there until King Herod died. This made the words that the Lord had spoken through the prophet come true: "I called my son out of Egypt."

When Herod realized that the wise men had tricked him, he became very angry. He gave orders to kill all the boys two years old and younger who were living in Bethlehem and the area around it. This was because the wise men had first seen the star two years earlier. This made the words of Jeremiah the prophet come true. He had said, "A voice is heard in Ramah, the sound of crying and deep sadness. Rachel is crying over her children and she refuses to be comforted, because they are gone."

After this Herod died, and Joseph, who was still in Egypt, had a dream. An angel of the Lord appeared to him and said, "Get up! Take the child and his mother and go back to the land of Israel, because the people who were trying to kill him are dead." So Joseph got up and took the child and his mother back to the land of Israel. But when he learned that Archelaus had succeeded his father Herod as king of Judea, he was afraid to go there. He was warned in a dream, and he went back to the land of Galilee instead. There he lived in a town called Nazareth. The prophets had said that Jesus would be called a Nazarene, and in this way their words came true. Matt. 2:1-23

There the child grew and became strong; he was filled with wisdom and blessed by God's grace.

Every year Jesus' parents would go to Jerusalem for the Passover Feast. When Jesus was 12 years old, they went up to the feast as usual. After the feast was over, they left to go back home. The boy Jesus stayed behind in Jerusalem, but they didn't realize this; they thought he was traveling with others in their group. So they went on for a day. Then they began to look for him among their relatives and friends, and when they didn't find him, they went back to Jerusalem to look for him. After three days they found him in the temple courtyard. He was sitting with the teachers, listening to them and asking them questions. Everyone who heard him was astonished by how much he understood and the answers he gave. When his parents saw him, they were shocked. His mother said to him, "Son, why have you treated us like this? Your father and I have been worried about you. We've been looking for you everywhere."

"Why were you looking for me?" he replied. "Didn't you know I had to be in my Father's house?" But they didn't understand what he meant by that. Then he returned to Nazareth with them and was obedient to them. But his mother kept all these things like a secret treasure in her heart.

Jesus became wiser and stronger, and he pleased both God and all the people more and more. Luke 2:40-52

CHAPTER 3

PREPARING THE WAY

There was a man sent from God whose name was John. He came to be a witness about the light so that all people might believe. John himself was not the light; he only came as a witness to the light. John 1:6-8 God's word came to John, the son of Zechariah, in the desert. He went into all the countryside around the Jordan River, preaching that people should be baptized and turn away from their sins so that God would forgive them. Luke 3:2-3

John is the one Isaiah the prophet was talking about when he said, "A messenger is calling out in the desert, 'Prepare the way for the Lord, make straight paths for him.'" John's clothes were made out of camel's hair, and he wore a leather belt around his waist. For food, he ate locusts and wild honey. People came out to him from Jerusalem, all of Judea, and the whole area around the Jordan River. They confessed their sins, and John baptized them in the Jordan.

But when he saw many Pharisees and Sadducees coming to be baptized, John said to them, "You little snakes! Who warned you to try to escape the punishment that's coming? If you have turned away from your sins, you have to live in a way that shows that. Don't think you're safe just because you can say, 'We come from Abraham.' I tell you, God can raise up children for Abraham even from these stones. The ax is already at the tree roots, and any tree that doesn't produce good fruit will be cut down and thrown into the fire." Matt. 3:3-10

"Then what should we do?" asked the crowd.

John answered, "Anyone who has extra clothes should share them with those who have none, and anyone who has extra food should do the same."

Even tax collectors came to be baptized. "Teacher," they asked, "what should we do?"

"Don't collect any more than you're supposed to," John told them.

Then some soldiers asked him, "And what should we do?"

John replied, "Don't force people to give you money, don't bring false charges against anybody, and be content with your pay."

The people all believed that something great was about to happen. They were wondering in their hearts whether John was the Messiah. But John said to everyone, "I'm baptizing you with water, but someone is coming who's more powerful than I am. I'm not even worthy to untie the straps of his sandals. He will baptize you with the Holy Spirit and with fire."

John said many other things to warn the people and to announce the good news to them. Luke 3:10-18

Jesus was about 30 years old when he began his ministry. Luke 3:23 Jesus came from Galilee to the Jordan River so that John could baptize him. But John didn't want to. He told Jesus, "I need to be baptized by you, so why are you coming to me?"

Jesus answered, "Please agree to this. It's right for us to do everything that God is asking of people now." So then John agreed.

Right after Jesus was baptized, as he was coming up out of the water, at that moment, heaven was opened and Jesus saw the Spirit of God coming down on him like a dove. A voice from heaven said, "This is my beloved Son. I'm very pleased with him." Matt. 3:13-17

Then the Holy Spirit led Jesus into the desert, and there the devil tempted him. Jesus didn't eat for 40 days and 40 nights, and he got very hungry. The tempter [Satan] came to him and said, "If you are the Son of God, tell these stones to become bread."

Jesus answered, "It is written, 'People must not live only on bread, but on every word that comes from the mouth of God.' "

Then the devil took Jesus to the holy city and had him stand on the highest point of the temple. "If you are the Son of God," he said, "throw yourself down. After all, it is written, " 'The Lord will command his angels to take good care of you. They will lift you up in their hands so that you don't trip over a stone.' "

Jesus answered, "It is also written, 'Don't test the Lord your God.' "

Then the devil took Jesus to a very high mountain. He showed him all the kingdoms of the world and their glory. "If you bow down and worship me," he said, "I'll give you all this."

Jesus said to him, "Get away from me, Satan! It is written, 'Worship the Lord your God and serve only him.' "

Then the devil left Jesus, and angels came and took care of him. Matt. 4:1-11

When the Jewish leaders in Jerusalem sent priests and Levites to ask John who he was, he didn't deny anything; he admitted, "I'm not the Messiah."

"Then who are you?" they asked him. "Are you Elijah?"

"No, I'm not," he replied.

"Are you the Prophet we've been expecting?" they asked.

"No," he answered.

They asked one last time, "Then who are you? Give us an answer to take back to the people who sent us. Who do you say you are?"

John replied, using the words of Isaiah the prophet, "I'm the voice calling out in the desert, 'Make a straight way for the Lord.' "

The Pharisees who'd been sent asked him, "Why are you baptizing people if you're not the Messiah, or Elijah, or the Prophet we've been expecting?"

"I baptize people with water," John replied, "but there's someone already with you who's still unknown to you. He's the one who's going to come after me. I'm not even worthy to untie his sandals."

This all happened at Bethany on the other side of the Jordan River, where John was baptizing.

The next day John saw Jesus coming toward him. He said, "Look, the Lamb of God who takes away the sin of the world! This is the one I was talking about when I said, 'Someone is coming after me who came before me, because he was there before me.' I didn't know who he was, but I came and baptized with water so that Israel would find out who he was."

Then John told them, "I saw the Spirit come down from heaven like a dove and rest on him. I didn't know who it would be, but the one who sent me to baptize with water told me, 'When you see the Spirit come down and rest on someone, that's the one who will baptize with the Holy Spirit.' Now I've seen that, and I'm a witness that this is God's Chosen One." John 1:19-34

CHAPTER 4

JESUS STARTS HIS MISSION

The next day John was there again with two of his disciples. When he saw Jesus walking by, he said, "Look, the Lamb of God!"

When the two disciples heard him say that, they followed Jesus. When Jesus turned around and saw them following, he asked, "What do you want?"

"Rabbi," they answered, "where are you staying?" (Rabbi means Teacher.)

He replied, "Come and see."

So they went and saw where he was staying. They went at about four o'clock in the afternoon, and they spent the rest of the day with him.

Andrew, Simon Peter's brother, was one of the two disciples who heard what John said and followed Jesus. The first thing Andrew did was find his brother Simon and tell him, "We've found the Messiah!" (Messiah means Christ.) Andrew brought Simon to Jesus.

Jesus looked at him and said, "You're Simon, the son of John, but you'll be known as Cephas." (Cephas means Peter, or Rock.)

The next day Jesus decided to leave for Galilee. He found Philip and told him, "Follow me."

Philip was from the town of Bethsaida, like Andrew and Peter. Philip found Nathanael and told him, "We've found the one Moses wrote about in the Law. The prophets wrote about him too. It's Jesus of Nazareth, the son of Joseph."

"Nazareth!" Nathanael responded. "Can anything good come from there?"

"Come and see," Philip answered.

When Jesus saw Nathanael approaching, he said, "Here's a true Israelite. There is nothing fake about him."

"Where do you know me from?" Nathanael asked.

Jesus answered, "I saw you while you were still under the fig tree, before Philip called you."

Nathanael replied, "Rabbi, you're the Son of God! You're the king of Israel!"

Jesus said, "You believe because I told you that I saw you under the fig tree. You're going to see greater things than that." Then he said to the disciples, "Truly I tell you, you will see heaven open, and the angels of God ascending and descending on the Son of Man." John 1:35-51

Two days later there was a wedding at Cana in Galilee. Jesus' mother was there, and Jesus and his disciples were also invited to the wedding. When the wine ran out, Jesus' mother said to him, "They don't have any wine left."

"Dear woman, what's going on here?" Jesus responded. "My time hasn't come yet."

His mother said to the servants, "Do whatever he tells you."

There were six water jars nearby made from stone. The Jews used water from that kind of jar to wash themselves so that they would be pure and clean. Each jar could hold 20 to 30 gallons.

Jesus said to the servants, "Fill the jars with water." So they filled them right to the top.

Then he told them, "Now take some out and bring it to the person in charge of the banquet."

So they did what he said. The person in charge tasted the water that had been turned into wine, but he didn't know where it had come from, though the servants who brought the water knew. He called over the groom and said to him, "Everyone brings out their best wine first, and after the guests have been drinking for a while, then they bring out the cheaper wine. But you've saved the best until now."

What Jesus did at Cana in Galilee was the first of his signs showing his glory. Because of it, his disciples believed in him.

After that, Jesus went down to Capernaum with his mother and brothers and his disciples. They all stayed there for a few days. John 2:1-12

A Pharisee named Nicodemus, who was one of the Jewish leaders, came to see Jesus one night. He said, "Rabbi, we know that you're a teacher who has come from God, because no one could do the signs you're doing unless God was with them."

Jesus answered, "Truly I tell you, no one can see the kingdom of God unless they're born again."

"How can someone be born when they're old?" Nicodemus asked. "They can't go back inside their mother and be born a second time!"

Jesus answered, "Truly I tell you, no one can enter the kingdom of God unless they're born of water and the Spirit. People give birth to people, but the Spirit gives birth to spirit. You shouldn't be surprised when I tell you, 'You must all be born again.' The wind blows wherever it wants to. You hear the sound it makes, but you can't tell where it's coming from or where it's going. It's the same with everyone who's born of the Spirit."

"How can this be?" Nicodemus asked.

Jesus answered, "You're Israel's teacher, but you don't understand these things? Truly I tell you, we speak about what we know, and we're witnesses about what we've seen. But you people still don't accept our testimony. I've spoken to you about earthly things, and you haven't believed. So how will you believe if I speak about heavenly things? No one has ever gone into heaven except the Son of Man who came from heaven. Just as Moses lifted up the snake in the desert, the Son of Man must also be lifted up so that everyone who believes may have eternal life in him.

"God loved the world so much that he gave his one and only Son so that anyone who believes in him may not die but have eternal life. God didn't send his Son into the world to judge the world, but to save the world through him. Anyone who believes in him is not judged, but anyone who doesn't believe is already judged, because they haven't believed in the name of God's one and only Son. This is the verdict: Light has come into the world, but people loved darkness rather than light because they were doing what was wrong. Everyone who does wrong hates the light and doesn't come into the light, because they're afraid that what they're doing will get them in trouble. But anyone who lives by the truth comes into the light so that it will be clear that they're doing what God wants."

After this, Jesus and his disciples went out into the countryside of Judea. They spent some time together there and baptized people. John was also baptizing, at Aenon near Salim, because there was plenty of water there and people were coming to be baptized. (This was before John was put in prison.)

An argument about special washings broke out between John's disciples and a certain Jewish man. The disciples came to John and said, "Rabbi, everyone is going to that man who was with you on the other side of the Jordan River. You were a witness about who he was, and now he's here baptizing people."

John replied, "A person can receive only what is given to them from heaven. You yourselves heard me say, 'I'm not the Messiah, I was sent ahead of him.' The bride belongs to the groom. The friend who helps the groom waits and listens for him, and he's filled with joy when he hears the groom's voice. That joy is mine, and now it is complete. He must become greater; I must become less.

"The one who comes from above is above everything. The one who is from the earth belongs to the earth and speaks like someone from the earth. The one who comes from heaven is above everything. He is a witness to what he has seen and heard, but no one accepts what he says. Anyone who does accept it acknowledges that God is true. The one that God has sent speaks God's words, because God gives the Spirit without limit. The Father loves the Son and has entrusted everything to him. Whoever believes in the Son has eternal life, but whoever who does not obey the Son will not see life, because God's anger remains on them." John 3:1-36

Jesus had to go through Samaria. He came to a town there called Sychar, near the piece of land Jacob had given his son Joseph. Jacob's well was there. Jesus was tired from the journey, so he sat down by the well. It was around noon.

A woman from Samaria came to get some water. Jesus said to her, "Please give me something to drink." (His disciples had gone into the town to buy food.)

The Samaritan woman replied, "You're a Jew, and I'm a Samaritan woman. How can you ask me for a drink?" (She said this because Jews won't have anything to do with Samaritans.)

Jesus answered, "If you knew the gift of God and who was asking you for a drink, you would have asked him, and he would have given you living water."

"Sir," the woman said, "you don't have any jar, and the well is deep. Where would you get this living water? Are you greater than our father Jacob, who gave us this well? He drank from it himself, and so did his sons and his animals."

Jesus answered, "Everyone who drinks this water will get thirsty again. But anyone who drinks the water I give them will never get thirsty. In fact, the water I give them will become a spring of water inside them bubbling up into eternal life."

The woman said to him, "Sir, give me that water so that I won't get thirsty and I won't have to keep coming here to get water!"

He told her, "Go get your husband and come back."

"I don't have a husband," she answered.

Jesus said to her, "You're right to say that you don't have a husband. You've had five husbands, and the man you're living with now isn't your husband. What you've just said is very true."

"Sir," the woman said, "I can tell that you're a prophet. Our people have always worshiped on this mountain, but you Jews claim that the place where we should worship is in Jerusalem."

Jesus said, "Woman, believe me, a time is coming when you won't worship the Father either on this mountain or in Jerusalem. You Samaritans worship what you don't know; we worship what we do know, because salvation comes from the Jews. But a time is coming— in fact, it's already here—when true worshipers will worship the Father in the Spirit and in truth. Those are the kind of worshipers the Father is looking for. God is spirit, and his worshipers must worship him in the Spirit and in truth."

The woman said, "I know that the Messiah is coming, the one called the Christ. When he comes, he'll explain everything to us."

Then Jesus said, "That's the one who's talking to you. It's me."

Just then Jesus' disciples came back, and they were surprised to find him talking with a woman. But no one asked her, "What do you want?" And no one asked him, "Why are you talking with her?"

The woman left her water jar and went back to the town. She told the people, "Come and see a man who told me everything I've ever done. Could this be the Messiah?" The people came out from the town and made their way toward Jesus.

Meanwhile, his disciples were telling him, "Rabbi, eat something!"

But he said to them, "I have food to eat that you don't know anything about."

Then his disciples asked each other, "Did someone bring him food?"

"My food," Jesus said, "is to do what my Father sent me to do and to finish his work."

Many of the Samaritans from that town believed in Jesus because of what the woman said about him: "He told me everything I've ever done." The people came to him and asked him to stay with them, so he stayed for two days. And many more of them believed as he spoke with them.

They told the woman, "At first we believed because of what you said. But now we've heard for ourselves, and we know that this man really is the Savior of the world."

After those two days Jesus left and continued on to Galilee. (He himself had pointed out that a prophet isn't respected in his own country.) When he arrived in Galilee, the people living there welcomed him. They'd seen everything he'd done in Jerusalem at the Passover Feast because they'd been there themselves.

Jesus went again to Cana in Galilee, where he had turned the water into wine. A royal official was there whose son was sick in bed at Capernaum. When he heard that Jesus had arrived in Galilee from Judea, he went to Jesus and begged him to come and heal his son. The boy was close to death.

Jesus told him, "You people will never believe unless you see signs and wonders."

The royal official said, "Sir, please come before my child dies."

"You may go home," Jesus replied. "Your son will live."

The man took Jesus at his word and headed home. While he was still on the way, his slaves met him and told him that the boy was going to live. He asked them at what time his son had gotten better.

They replied, "Yesterday, at one o'clock in the afternoon, the fever left him."

Then the father realized that this was the exact time when Jesus had said to him, "Your son will live." He and his whole family became believers.

This was the second sign that Jesus did. He did it after he came back from Judea to Galilee. John 4:4-34, 39-54

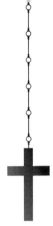

CHAPTER 5

OPPOSITION BEGINS

Jesus went to Nazareth, where he had been brought up. On the Sabbath day he went as usual to the synagogue and stood up to read. They handed him the scroll of Isaiah the prophet. Jesus unrolled it and found the right place. He read what was written there: "The Spirit of the Lord is on me, because he has anointed me to announce the good news to the poor. He has sent me to announce freedom for prisoners, to make the blind see again, to set free those who are mistreated, and to say that this is the time when God will act."

Then Jesus rolled up the scroll, gave it back to the attendant, and sat down. Everyone in the synagogue had their eyes on him. He began by telling them, "Today this passage of Scripture has come true as you have listened."

Everyone said good things about him. They were amazed at the gracious words they heard from his lips. "Isn't this Joseph's son?" they asked.

Jesus responded, "You'll certainly apply this saying to me: 'Doctor, heal yourself!' And by that you'll mean, 'We want you to do here in your hometown the things we've heard you did in Capernaum.' Truly I tell you a prophet is not accepted in his own hometown."

All the people in the synagogue became very angry when they heard these things. They got up, ran Jesus out of town, and took him to the edge of the hill on which the town was built. They were planning to throw him off the cliff, but Jesus walked right through the crowd and went on his way. Luke 4:16-24, 28-30

One day when Jesus was standing by the Sea of Galilee, all the people crowded around him to listen to the word of God. At the edge of the water, Jesus saw two boats. They had been left there by the fishermen, who were washing their nets. He got into one of the boats, which belonged to a man named Simon. Jesus asked him to pull out a little way from shore. Then he sat down in the boat and taught the people.

When Jesus had finished speaking, he turned to Simon and said, "Go out into the deep water and let down the nets so you can catch some fish."

Simon answered, "Master, we worked hard all night, but we didn't catch anything. However, because you say so, I will let down the nets."

When they did so, they caught a large number of fish—so many that their nets began to break! They quickly signaled to their partners in the other boat to come and help them. They came, and together they filled both boats so full that they nearly sank.

When Simon Peter saw this, he fell at Jesus' knees. "Go away from me, Lord!" he said. "I'm a sinful man!" He and his crew were amazed at the number of fish they'd caught, and so were his partners, James and John, the sons of Zebedee.

Then Jesus said to Simon, "Don't be afraid, from now on you will fish for people."

So they pulled their boats up on shore, left everything, and followed him. Luke 5:1-11

They went to Capernaum, and when the Sabbath day came, Jesus went into the synagogue and began to teach. The people were amazed at his teaching, because he taught them with authority, not like the teachers of the law.

Just then a man in the synagogue who was controlled by an evil spirit cried out, "What do you want with us, Jesus of Nazareth? Have you come to destroy us? I know who you are. You're the Holy One of God!"

"Be quiet!" Jesus ordered the spirit. "Come out of him!" The evil spirit shook the man wildly and came out of him with a scream.

All the people were amazed and asked each other, "What is this? A new teaching—and with such authority! He even gives orders to evil spirits, and they obey him."

News about Jesus spread quickly all over Galilee.

Jesus left the synagogue and went with James and John to the home of Simon and Andrew. Simon's mother-in-law was sick in bed with a fever, and they told Jesus about her as soon as he came in. He went to her, took her hand, and helped her up. Then the fever left her, and she began to serve them.

That evening after sunset the people brought Jesus everyone who was sick or controlled by demons. The whole town gathered at the door, and Jesus healed many people who had different kinds of sicknesses. He also drove out many demons, but he wouldn't permit the demons to speak, because they knew who he was.

Very early in the morning, while it was still dark, Jesus got up and left the house. He went to a place where he could be alone and pray. Simon and his friends went looking for Jesus, and when they found him, they told him, "Everyone is looking for you!"

Jesus answered, "Let's leave this place and go to the towns nearby so I can preach there too. That's why I've come." Mark 1:21-38

Jesus went all over Galilee, teaching in the synagogues, preaching the good news of the kingdom, and healing every illness and sickness that the people had. News about him spread all over Syria, and they brought him everyone who was ill with any kind of sicknesses. Some were suffering great pain, while others were controlled by demons.

Some were shaking wildly, and others couldn't move at all. Jesus healed every one of them. Large crowds followed him from Galilee, from the area known as the Ten Cities, from Jerusalem and Judea, and from the area across the Jordan River. Matt. 4:23-25

While Jesus was in one of the towns, a man came along who had a skin disease all over his body. When the man saw Jesus, he fell with his face to the ground and begged him, "Lord, you can make me clean, if you are willing."

Jesus reached out his hand and touched the man. "I am willing," he said. "Be clean!" Right away the disease left him.

"Don't tell anyone," Jesus ordered him. "But go and show yourself to the priest and offer the sacrifices that Moses commanded, as a witness to the priest and the people that you are clean."

But the news about Jesus spread even more, so that crowds of people came to hear him and to be healed of their sicknesses. But Jesus often went away to be by himself and pray.

One day when Jesus was teaching, some Pharisees and teachers of the law were among those sitting there and listening to him. They'd come from every village in Galilee and from Judea and Jerusalem. The power of the Lord was with Jesus to heal the sick. Some men brought a man who couldn't walk. They were carrying him on a mat. They tried to take him into the house and set him in front of Jesus, but they couldn't get in because of the crowd. So they went up onto the roof and made an opening in the tiles. Then they lowered the man on his mat down into the middle of the crowd, right in front of Jesus.

When Jesus saw how much faith they had, he said to the man, "Friend, your sins are forgiven."

The Pharisees and the teachers of the law began to think, "Who is this person who says such an evil thing? Only God can forgive sins!"

But Jesus knew what they were thinking and asked, "Why are you thinking these things in your hearts? Which is easier to say, 'Your sins are forgiven,' or, 'Get up and walk'? But I want you to know that the Son of Man has authority on earth to forgive sins." So he said to the man who couldn't walk, "I tell you, get up, take your mat, and go home." Right away the man stood up in front of them. He picked up his mat and went home praising God. Everyone was astounded and gave glory to God. They were filled with wonder and said, "We've seen amazing things today!" Luke 5:12-26

As Jesus went on from there, he saw a man named Matthew sitting at a tax collection booth. "Follow me," Jesus told him. So Matthew got up and followed him.

Jesus went to have dinner at Matthew's house, and many tax collectors and sinners came and ate with him and his disciples. When the Pharisees saw this, they asked the disciples, "Why does your teacher eat with tax collectors and sinners?"

When Jesus heard this, he responded, "Those who are healthy don't need a doctor. Sick people do. Go and learn what this means, 'I want mercy and not sacrifice.' I haven't come to call those who are right with God. I've come for sinners." Matt. 9:9-13

Some of the people who were there said to Jesus, "John's disciples often pray and go without eating, and so do the Pharisees' disciples. But yours go on eating and drinking."

Jesus answered, "Would you ask a bridegroom's friends to fast during his wedding celebration? But the time will come when the groom is taken away from them, and in those days, they will go without eating."

Then Jesus gave them an illustration. He said, "No one tears a piece out of a new garment to patch an old one. That would ruin the new garment, and the patch wouldn't match the old one anyway. And nobody pours new wine into old wineskins. The new wine would burst the skins, so the wine would spill everywhere, and the wineskins would also be ruined. No, new wine has to be poured into new wineskins. But after drinking old wine, no one wants the new. They say, 'The old wine is better.'" Luke 5:33-39

Some time later, Jesus went up to Jerusalem for one of the Jewish feasts. In Jerusalem near the Sheep Gate there's a pool that's called Bethesda in the Hebrew language. It's surrounded by five rows of columns that have a roof over them. A great number of people who were disabled used to lie down by that pool. These included people who were blind, who couldn't walk, and who could hardly move. One man was there who hadn't been able to walk for 38 years.

When Jesus saw him lying there and found out that he'd been in that condition for a long time, he asked him, "Do you want to get better?"

"Sir," the disabled man replied, "I don't have anyone to help me into the pool when the water starts rippling. I try to get in, but someone else always gets in ahead of me."

Then Jesus told him, "Get up! Pick up your mat and walk." The man was healed at once, and he picked up his mat and started to walk away.

But this happened on a Sabbath day, so the Jewish leaders said to the man who'd been healed, "It's the Sabbath day. The law doesn't allow you to carry your mat today."

But he replied, "The man who healed me told me, 'Pick up your mat and walk.'"

They asked him, "What man was that? Who told you to pick it up and walk?"

The man who'd been healed had no idea who it was, because Jesus had slipped away into the crowd that was there.

Later Jesus found him at the temple and told him, "Now that you're well again, don't sin anymore, or something worse might happen to you."

The man went away and told the Jewish leaders it was Jesus who had made him well.

Because Jesus was doing things like this on the Sabbath day, the Jewish leaders began to persecute him. Jesus said in his own defense,

"My Father is always at work right up to this day, and I am working too."

After he said that, the Jewish leaders wanted even more to kill him, because he wasn't just breaking the law for the Sabbath day. He was calling God his own Father, making himself equal with God.

Jesus answered, "Truly I tell you, the Son can do nothing by himself. He can do only what he sees his Father doing. Whatever the Father does, the Son also does, because the Father loves the Son and shows him everything that he's doing. Yes, and the Father will show the Son even greater things than these, so that you will be amazed. The Father raises the dead and gives them life; in the same way, the Son gives life to anyone he wishes. And the Father doesn't judge anyone; he has left it up to the Son to judge, so that all people will honor the Son just as they honor the Father. Whoever doesn't honor the Son doesn't honor the Father who sent him.

"Truly I tell you, whoever hears my word and believes in the one who sent me has eternal life. They will not be judged, because they have crossed over from death into life. Truly I tell you, a time is coming—and in fact, it has already come—when the dead will hear the voice of the Son of God, and those who hear it will live. The Father has life in himself, and he has given the Son life in his own self as well. And because he is the Son of Man, the Father has also given him the authority to judge.

"Don't be amazed at this. You'll see I'm telling the truth when all who are in their graves will hear his voice and come out. Those who have done what is good will rise to live again, and those who have done wrong will rise to face judgment. I can do nothing by myself. I judge only as I hear, and I judge fairly, because I don't try to please myself. I try to please the one who sent me.

"If I'm being a witness for myself, you don't know whether to trust me. But there's someone else who's a witness in my favor, and I know that what he says about me is trustworthy. You've sent people to John, and he has been a witness to the truth. I don't depend on human testimony, but I mention John's witness so that you can be saved. John was like a lamp that burned and gave light, and you chose to enjoy his light for a while.

"I have a witness even greater than John. The works the Father has given me to finish—the very works that I'm doing—are a witness that the Father has sent me. And the Father who sent me is a witness about me himself. You've never heard his voice, and you've never seen what he really looks like, and his word doesn't live in you, because you don't believe the one he has sent. You study the Scriptures carefully because you think they will give you eternal life. The same Scriptures you study are also a witness about me. But you still refuse to come to me and receive life.

"I don't accept praise from human beings, and I know that you don't have the love of God in your hearts. I've come in my Father's name, and you haven't accepted me. But if someone else comes in his own name, you accept him. You accept praise from one another, but you don't seek the praise that comes from the only God. So how can you believe"? John 5:1-44

One Sabbath day when Jesus was walking through some grain fields, his disciples began to break off heads of grain, rub them in their hands, and eat them.

Some of the Pharisees said, "It's against the Law to do that on the Sabbath day. Why are you doing it?"

Jesus answered, "Haven't you ever read what David did? When he and his men were hungry, he went into the house of God and took the holy bread. He ate the bread that only priests were allowed to eat, and he even gave it to his men." Then Jesus said to them, "The Son of Man is Lord of the Sabbath day."

On another Sabbath day, Jesus went into the synagogue and began teaching. A man was there whose right hand was weak and twisted. The Pharisees and the teachers of the law wanted to have something they could hold against Jesus, so they watched him closely to see if he would heal on the Sabbath day. But Jesus knew what they were thinking. He said to the man who had the weak and twisted hand, "Get up and stand in front of everyone." So the man got up and stood there.

Then Jesus said to them, "What does the Law say we should do on the Sabbath day? Should we do good, or should we do evil? Should we save life, or should we destroy it?"

He looked around at all of them. Then he said to the man, "Stretch out your hand." He did this, and his hand was made as good as new.

But the Pharisees and the teachers of the law got very angry. They began to talk to one another about what they could do to Jesus. Luke 6:1-11

CHAPTER 6

TEACHING THE PEOPLE

Jesus went off to the Sea of Galilee with his disciples, and a large crowd from Galilee followed him. When people heard about everything he was doing, many others also came to him from Judea, Jerusalem, Idumea, and the areas east of the Jordan River and around Tyre and Sidon. Because the crowd was so big, Jesus told his disciples to get a small boat ready for him so the people wouldn't crush him. Jesus had healed many people, so those who were still sick were pushing forward to try to touch him.

Whenever evil spirits saw him, they fell down in front of him and shouted, "You are the Son of God!" But Jesus ordered them not to tell anyone about him. Mark 3:7-12 This was to make what the prophet Isaiah had said come true: "Here is my servant, the one I have chosen. He's the one I love, and I'm very pleased with him. I will put my Spirit on him, and he'll announce to the nations that everything is going to be made right. He won't argue or cry out; no one will hear his voice in the streets. He won't break a bent twig, and he won't snuff out a smoldering wick. He'll make right win over wrong, and the nations will put their hope in him." Matt. 12:17-21

On one of those days, Jesus went up onto a mountainside to pray. He spent the whole night praying to God. When morning came, he called his disciples together and chose 12 of them to be apostles. Here are their names: Simon, whom Jesus named Peter, and his brother Andrew, James, John, Philip, Bartholomew, Matthew, Thomas, James the son of Alphaeus, Simon, who was called the Zealot, Judas, the son of James, and Judas Iscariot, who later handed Jesus over to his enemies. Luke 6:12-16

Later, when Jesus saw the crowds, he went up on a mountainside and sat down. His disciples came to him, and he began to teach them. He said,

> "Blessed are the poor in spirit, because the kingdom of heaven belongs to them.
> Blessed are those who mourn, because they will be comforted.
> Blessed are those who are humble, because they will inherit the earth.
> Blessed are those who are hungry and thirsty for justice, because they will be fully satisfied.
> Blessed are those who show mercy, because they will be shown mercy.
> Blessed are those who have pure hearts, because they will see God.
> Blessed are those who make peace, because they will be called children of God.
> Blessed are those who suffer for the sake of justice, because the kingdom of heaven is theirs. Matt. 5:1-10
> Blessed are you when people hate you, when they have nothing to do with you, when they say bad things about you, and when they treat your name as evil because of the Son of Man.

"The prophets of long ago were treated in the same way. So when these things happen to you, be glad and jump for joy. You will receive many blessings in heaven.

"But woe to you who are rich! You've already had your easy life.
Woe to you who are well fed now! You will go hungry.
Woe to you who laugh now! You will cry and be sad.
Woe to you when everyone says good things about you! That's
how they treated the false prophets long ago. Luke 6:22-26

"You're the salt of the earth. But if salt loses its saltiness, how can it be made salty again? It's not good for anything anymore. It has to be thrown out onto the street.

"You're the light of the world. A city that's built on top of a hill can't be hidden. People don't light a lamp and then put it under a bowl. Instead, they put it on a stand so that it gives light to everyone in the house. In the same way, let your light shine so that others can see it. Then they'll see the good things you do and praise your Father who is in heaven.

"Don't think that I've come to set aside what's written in the Law and the Prophets. I haven't come to do that, but to fulfill what's written. Truly I tell you, heaven and earth will disappear before the smallest letter disappears from the Law. Not even the smallest mark of a pen will disappear until everything the Law says happens. So anyone who sets aside one of the least of the commands and teaches others to do the same will be called the least in the kingdom of heaven. But anyone who practices and teaches the commands will be called great in the kingdom of heaven. I tell you, unless your righteousness is even better than the righteousness of the Pharisees and the teachers of the law, you won't enter the kingdom of heaven.

"You've heard that it was said to the people long ago, 'Don't commit murder. Anyone who commits murder will answer for it in court.' But I tell you that anyone who loses their temper with a brother or sister will answer for it in court. Anyone who speaks scornfully to a brother or sister will face the council of elders. And anyone who dismisses someone as worthless will be in danger of the fire in hell. Suppose you're offering your gift at the altar and you remember that your brother or sister has something against you. Leave your gift in front of the altar, go and make peace with them, and then come back and offer your gift.

"Suppose someone has a claim against you and is taking you to court. Settle the matter quickly, while you're still on the way there together. If you don't, you may be handed over to the judge, the judge may hand you over to the officer, and you may be thrown into prison. Truly I tell you, then you won't get out until you've paid the very last penny!

"You've heard that it was said, 'Do not commit adultery.' But I tell you that anyone who looks with lust at a woman has already committed adultery with her in his heart. If your right eye causes you to sin, pull it out and throw it away. It's better to lose one part of your body than for your whole body to be thrown into hell. If your right hand causes you to sin, cut it off and throw it away. It's better to lose one part of your body than for your whole body to be thrown into hell.

"It has been said, 'Any man who divorces his wife must give her a letter of divorce.' But I tell you that anyone who divorces his wife for any reason other than unfaithfulness makes her a victim of adultery. And anyone who marries a divorced woman commits adultery.

"Again, you've heard that it was said to the people long ago, 'Don't break your promises. Keep the promises you make to the Lord.' But I tell you, don't make any promises like that. Don't make them in the name of heaven, because that's God's throne. Don't make them in the name of the earth, because that's where God rests his feet. Don't make them in the name of Jerusalem, because that's the city of the Great King. And don't guarantee a promise with your own head, because you can't turn even one hair of your head white or black. All you need to say is simply 'yes' or 'no.' Anything more than that comes from the evil one.

"You've heard that it was said, 'An eye for an eye and a tooth for a tooth.' But I tell you not to retaliate against someone who treats you poorly. Suppose someone slaps you on your right cheek. Then turn your other cheek to them as well. Suppose someone takes you to court to get your shirt. Let them have your coat too. Suppose someone forces you to go one mile. Go two miles with them. If a person asks you for something, give it to them, and if a person wants to borrow something from you, let them borrow it.

"You've heard that it was said, 'Love your neighbor. Hate your enemy.' But I tell you, love your enemies, and pray for those who hurt you. That way you'll be the children of your Father who is in heaven. He causes his sun to shine on bad people and good people, and he sends rain on those who do right and those who don't. Matt. 5:13-45

"Suppose you love those who love you. Should anyone praise you for that? Even sinners love those who love them. Suppose you do good to those who are good to you. Should anyone praise you? Even sinners do the same. And suppose you lend money to those who can pay you back. Should anyone praise you? Even sinners lend to sinners, expecting them to pay everything back. But love your enemies, do good to them, and lend to them without expecting to get anything back. Then you will have a great reward. You will be children of the Most High God, who is kind to people who do wrong and are ungrateful. Show mercy to others, just as your Father shows mercy. Luke 6:32-36

"Be careful not to do good deeds in front of other people so that they'll see you. If you do that, you won't get any reward from your Father in heaven. When you give to people in need, don't announce it by having trumpets blown in front of you. That's what the hypocrites do in the synagogues and on the streets because they want people to notice them. Truly I tell you, that's all the reward they'll get. But when you give to people in need, don't let your left hand know what your right hand is doing. Then your Father, who sees what you do in secret, will reward you.

"When you pray, don't be like the hypocrites who love to stand and pray in the synagogues and on the street corners so that other people will see them. Truly I tell you, that's all the reward they'll get. When you pray, go into your room, close the door, and pray to your Father, who can't be seen. Then your Father, who sees what you do in secret, will reward you. And when you pray, don't keep talking on and on like the people who worship other gods. They think their prayers will be answered because they've talked so much. Don't be like them, because your Father knows what you need even before you ask him. Therefore, pray like this:

> Our Father in heaven, may your name be honored.
> May your kingdom come.
> May your will be done on earth as it already is done in heaven.
> Give us today our daily bread.
> And forgive our sins, just as we forgive those who sin against us.
> Don't let us fall into temptation.
> And save us from the evil one.

"If you forgive other people when they sin against you, your heavenly Father will also forgive you. But if you don't forgive other people, your Father won't forgive your sins.

"When you go without eating, don't look all sad like the hypocrites. They make strange faces so that people will notice that they're fasting. Truly I tell you, that's all the reward they'll get. But when you go without eating, refresh your hair with olive oil and wash your face. Then no one will be able to tell that you're fasting. Only your Father, who can't be seen, will know it. And your Father, who sees what you do in secret, will reward you.

"Don't try to get a lot of riches on earth, because moths and pests can destroy your things there, and thieves can break in and steal them. Instead, make sure you have a lot of riches in heaven, because moths and pests can't destroy anything there, and thieves can't break in and steal anything. Wherever your riches are, that's where your heart will be.

"The eye lets light into the body. If your eyes are healthy, your whole body will be full of light. But if your eyes are unhealthy, then your whole body will be full of darkness. If the light inside you is darkness, then it's really dark!

"No one can serve two masters. Either you'll hate the first and love the second, or you'll be devoted to the first and not care about the second. You can't serve both God and money. So I'm telling you not to worry about your life, what you'll eat or drink, and not to worry about your body, what you'll wear. Isn't there more to life than eating? And isn't there more to the body than clothes? Look at the birds of the air. They don't plant or harvest crops, and they don't put grain away in barns. But your heavenly Father feeds them. Aren't you worth much more than they are? Can any of you add even one hour to your life by worrying?

"And why do you worry about clothes? See how the wildflowers grow. They don't work or make clothes, but I tell you that not even Solomon in all his royal robes was dressed as well as one of these flowers. If God dresses the wild grass so well, even though it's here today and thrown into the fire tomorrow, isn't he even more likely to make sure that you have clothes?

"You have such little faith! Don't get all worried and say, 'What will we eat? What will we drink? What will we wear?' People who don't trust in God are concerned with those things. But your heavenly Father knows that you need them. So be concerned about the kingdom of God first, and do what he wants you to do, and all those things will also be given to you. Don't worry about tomorrow, let it worry about itself. Each day has enough troubles of its own. Matt. 6:1-34

"Don't judge other people, or you'll be judged yourself. You will be judged in the same way that you judge others, and the measure you use for others will be used for you. "Why do you look at the bit of sawdust in your friend's eye but pay no attention to the chunk of wood in your own eye? How can you say to your friend, 'Let me take the bit of sawdust out of your eye,' when there's a log in your own eye? You hypocrite! First take the piece of wood out of your own eye, and then you'll be able to see to take the bit of sawdust out of your friend's eye.

"Ask, and it will be given to you. Seek, and you will find. Knock, and the door will be opened to you. For everyone who asks receives, the one who seeks finds, and the door will be opened to anyone who knocks. "Suppose your son asks for bread. Which of you would give him a stone? Or suppose he asks for a fish. Which of you would give him a snake? Even people who are bad know how to give good gifts to their children. How much more will your heavenly Father give good gifts to those who ask him!

"In everything, do to others what you would want them to do to you. That sums up the Law and the Prophets.

"Enter through the narrow gate. The gate is large and the road is wide that leads to ruin. Many people go that way. But the gate is small and the road is narrow that leads to life. Only a few people find it.

"Watch out for false prophets. They come to you disguised as sheep, but on the inside they're hungry wolves. You'll recognize them by their fruit. Do people pick grapes from thorn bushes, or figs from thistles? In the same way, every good tree bears good fruit, but a bad tree bears bad fruit. A good tree can't bear bad fruit, and a bad tree can't bear good fruit. Every tree that doesn't bear good fruit is cut down and thrown into the fire. So you'll recognize them by their fruit. Matt. 7:1-20

"A good person says good things that come from the good stored up in their heart, but a bad person says bad things that come from the evil stored up in their heart, because a person's mouth says whatever's in their heart.

"Why do you call me, 'Lord, Lord,' but not do what I say? Luke 6:45-46 "Not everyone who says to me, 'Lord, Lord,' will enter the kingdom of heaven, but only those who do the will of my Father in heaven. Many will say to me on that day, 'Lord! Lord! Didn't we prophesy in your name? Didn't we drive out demons? Didn't we do many miracles?' But I will tell them outright, 'I never knew you. Get away from me—you didn't follow God's ways!'

"So then, everyone who hears my words and puts them into practice is like a wise person who built a house on a rock. The rain came down, the water rose, and the winds blew and beat against that house, but it didn't fall, because it was built on a rock.

"Everyone who hears my words but doesn't put them into practice is like a foolish person who built a house on the sand. The rain came down, the water rose, and the winds blew and beat against that house, and it fell with a loud crash."

When Jesus had finished saying all these things, the crowds were amazed at his teaching. He taught like one who had authority, and not like their teachers of the law. Matt. 7:21-29

CHAPTER 7

ACCUSED OF USING EVIL POWERS

Jesus finished saying all these things to the people who were listening, and then he went into Capernaum. A Roman commander there had a servant who was sick and about to die. His master thought highly of him, so when he heard about Jesus, he sent some of the Jewish elders to ask him to come and heal his servant. They went to Jesus and begged him, "This man deserves to have you do this, because he loves our nation and has built our synagogue." So Jesus went with them.

When Jesus came near the house, the Roman commander sent some of his friends to him. He told them to say, "Lord, don't trouble yourself. I'm not good enough to have you come into my house. I didn't even feel I was fit to come to you. But just say the word and my servant will be healed. I myself am under authority, and I have soldiers who obey my orders. I tell this one, 'Go,' and he goes. I tell that one, 'Come,' and he comes. I say to my servant, 'Do this,' and he does it."

When Jesus heard this, he was amazed at the commander. Jesus turned to the crowd that was following him and said, "I tell you, I haven't found anyone even in Israel whose faith is this strong." Then the men who'd been sent to Jesus returned to the house and found that the servant had been healed.

Some time later, Jesus went to a town called Nain. His disciples and a large crowd went along with him. Just as he approached the town gate, a dead person was being carried out. He was the only son of his mother, and she was a widow. A large crowd from the town was with her. When the Lord saw her, he felt compassion for her and said, "Don't cry."

Then he went up and touched the coffin. The people who were carrying it stood still. Jesus said, "Young man, I tell you, get up!" The man who had died sat up and started to talk, and Jesus gave him back to his mother.

All the people were filled with wonder, and they praised God. "A great prophet has appeared among us!" they said. "God has come to help his people." This news about Jesus spread throughout Judea and the whole country.

John's disciples told him about all these things. So he chose two of them and sent them to the Lord to ask him, "Are you the one who is supposed to come, or should we look for someone else?"

When the men got to Jesus they said, "John the Baptist sent us to ask you, 'Are you the one who is supposed to come, or should we look for someone else?'"

At that time Jesus healed many people who had illnesses, sicknesses, and evil spirits, and he restored the sight of many who were blind. Then Jesus replied to the messengers, "Go back to John and tell him what you have seen and heard: People who are blind receive their sight, those who are disabled walk, those with skin diseases are made clean, those who are deaf hear, those who have died are restored to life, and the good news is announced to the poor. Blessed is anyone who does not give up their faith because of me."

Then John's messengers left, and Jesus began to speak to the crowd about him. He said, "What did you go out into the desert to see? Tall grass waving in the wind? If not that, then what did you go out to see? A man dressed in fine clothes? No, those who wear fine clothes and live in luxury are found in palaces. Then what did you go out to see? A prophet? Yes, I tell you, and more than a prophet. He is the one written about in Scripture where it says, "'I will send my messenger ahead of you, and he will prepare your way for you.' I tell you, no one more important than John has ever been born. But the least important person in God's kingdom is more important than John."

When all the people, including the tax collectors, heard Jesus' words, they agreed that God's way was right, because they'd all been baptized by John. But the Pharisees and the experts in the law rejected God's purpose for themselves, because they hadn't been baptized by John.

Jesus went on to say, "What can I compare today's people to? What are they like? They're like children sitting in the market and calling out to each other who say, " 'We played the flute for you, but you didn't dance. So we sang a funeral song, but you didn't cry.' When John the Baptist came, he didn't eat bread or drink wine, and you said, 'He has a demon.' But when the Son of Man came, he did eat and drink, but you said, 'He always eats and drinks way too much, and he has tax collectors and sinners for friends.' But wisdom is proved right by all its followers." Luke 7:1-35

At that time Jesus said, "I praise you, Father, Lord of heaven and earth, because you've hidden these things from wise and educated people and shown them to little children. Yes, Father, you've done what you wanted to do.

"My Father has given everything to me. No one knows the Son except the Father. No one knows the Father except the Son—and anyone the Son chooses to show the Father to.

"Come to me, all you who are tired and carrying heavy loads, and I will give you rest. Become my servants and learn from me. I'm gentle and humble, and you'll find rest for your souls. My requirements are compassionate, and my load is light." Matt. 11:25-30

After this, Jesus traveled around from one town and village to another, announcing the good news of God's kingdom. His 12 disciples were with him, and so were some women who had been healed of evil spirits and sicknesses. One was Mary Magdalene; seven demons had come out of her. Another was Joanna, the wife of Chuza, the manager of Herod's household. A woman named Susanna and many others were also there. These women were using their own money to support Jesus and the 12 disciples. Luke 8:1-3

Then they brought Jesus a man who was controlled by demons that kept him from speaking or seeing. Jesus healed the man so that he could speak and see. All the people were amazed and asked, "Could this be the Son of David?"

But when the Pharisees heard this, they said, "This man drives out demons by the power of Beelzebul, the prince of demons."

Jesus knew what they were thinking, and he said to them, "Every kingdom that fights against itself will be destroyed. Every city or family that is divided against itself will not last. If Satan drives out Satan, he's fighting against himself, so how can his kingdom last? You say I drive out demons by the power of Beelzebul. Then by whose power do your own people drive them out? So then, they will be your judges. But if I drive out demons by the Spirit of God, then the kingdom of God is right here with you.

"Or think about this. You can't just walk into a strong man's house and take what he owns. You have to tie him up first, and then you can rob his house.

"Anyone who isn't with me is against me, and anyone who doesn't gather with me scatters. And so I tell you, every kind of sin and insult can be forgiven, but saying that the Holy Spirit is evil will not be forgiven. Anyone who speaks a word against the Son of Man will be forgiven, but anyone who speaks against the Holy Spirit will not be forgiven, either in this age or in the one to come." Matt. 12:22-32

As Jesus was saying these things, a woman in the crowd called out, "Blessed is the mother who gave you birth and nursed you."

He replied, "Blessed instead are those who hear God's word and obey it."

As the crowds were growing larger, Jesus told them, "The people of this generation are evil. They ask for a sign from God, but none will be given to them except the sign of Jonah. Just as he was a sign from God to the people of Nineveh, the Son of Man will be a sign from God to the people of today. Luke 11:27-30 Jonah was in the belly of a huge fish for three days and three nights, the Son of Man will spend three days and three nights in the grave. The people of Nineveh will stand up on judgment day with this generation and show that it's guilty. They turned away from their sins when Jonah preached to them, and now something greater than Jonah is here. The Queen of the South will stand up on judgment day with this generation and show that it's guilty. She came from far away to listen to Solomon's wisdom, and now something greater than Solomon is here.

"When an evil spirit comes out of a person, it goes through the deserts looking for a place to rest, but it doesn't find any. Then it says, 'I'll return to the house I just left.' When it gets back, it finds the house swept clean and put in order, with no one living in it. Then the evil spirit goes and gets seven other spirits that are even worse than it is, and they all go live there. Then the person is worse off than they were before. That's how it will be with this rebellious generation."

While Jesus was still talking to the crowd, his mother and brothers came and stood outside, wanting to speak to him. Someone told him, "Your mother and brothers are standing outside and they want to speak to you."

Jesus replied to him, "Who is my mother? And who are my brothers?" Pointing to his disciples, he said, "Here is my mother! Here are my brothers! Anyone who does what my heavenly Father wants is my brother and sister and mother." Matt. 12:40-50

Jesus went into another house, and such a large crowd gathered there that he and his disciples weren't even able to eat. When his family heard about this, they came to get him, because they thought, "He's out of his mind." Mark 3:20-21

That same day Jesus left the house and sat by the Sea of Galilee. The crowds that gathered around him were so large that he got into a boat and sat down to teach, while all the people stood on the shore to listen. Then he taught them many things by telling them stories.

He said, "A farmer went out to plant his seed. As he scattered it, some fell on a path and the birds came and ate it up. Some seed fell in rocky places where there wasn't much soil. Those plants came up quickly because the soil wasn't very deep. But when the sun got hot, it burned the plants and they dried up, because they had no roots. Other seed fell among thorns that grew up and crowded out the plants. But still other seed fell on good soil and produced a crop that was 100, 60, or 30 times more than what was planted. Whoever understands should take this to heart."

The disciples came to Jesus and asked, "Why do you tell stories when you speak to the people?"

He answered, "Because they aren't being given the knowledge of the secrets of the kingdom of heaven the way you are. Whoever has this kind of knowledge will be given more, until they have a great deal of it. But if anyone lacks this kind of knowledge, even what little they have will be taken away from them. I tell stories when I speak to the people so that: They'll look, but they won't see. They'll listen, but they won't hear or understand.

"These people are making the words of the prophet Isaiah come true. 'You'll hear but never understand, you'll see but never know what you're seeing. The hearts of these people have become stubborn. They can barely hear with their ears and they've closed their eyes. Otherwise they might see with their eyes, hear with their ears, and understand with their hearts. Then they might turn to the Lord, and he would heal them.'

"But blessed are your eyes, because they see, and blessed are your ears, because they hear. Truly I tell you, many prophets and godly people wanted to see what you're seeing, but they didn't see it, and they wanted to hear what you're hearing, but they didn't hear it." Matt. 13:1-17

Then Jesus said to them, "Don't you understand this story? Then how will you understand any of the stories? The seed that the farmer plants is God's message. Some of the seed that was scattered fell on a path. It stands for what happens when people hear the message but then Satan comes immediately and takes away what was planted in them. The seed that was scattered on rocky places represents other people who hear the message and right away receive it with joy. But because they have no roots, they last only a short time. When trouble or suffering comes because of the message, they quickly fall away from the faith. Still others, like the seed that was scattered among thorns, hear the message, but then the worries of this life, the false promises of wealth, and the desire for other things crowd out the message and keep it from producing fruit. And some people, like the seed that was scattered on good soil, hear the message, accept it, and produce a good crop that's 30, 60, or even 100 times more than what was planted." Mark 4:13-20

Jesus told the crowd another story. He said, "Here's what the kingdom of heaven is like. A man planted good seed in his field. But while everyone was sleeping, an enemy came, planted weeds among the wheat, and then slipped away. The wheat began to grow and form grain, but at the same time, weeds appeared.

"The owner's slaves came to him and said, 'Master, didn't you plant good seed in your field? Then where did these weeds come from?'

" 'An enemy must have done it,' he replied.

"The slaves asked him, 'Do you want us to go and pull up the weeds?'

" 'No,' the owner answered, 'because while you're pulling up the weeds, you might pull up the wheat too. Let them both grow together until the harvest. Then I'll tell the workers, "First collect the weeds and tie them in bundles to be burned. Then gather the wheat and put it in my barn." ' " Matt. 13:24-30

Jesus also said, "Here's what the kingdom of God is like. A farmer scatters seed on the ground. Night and day, whether he sleeps or gets up, the seed sprouts and grows. The farmer doesn't know how that happens. All by itself the soil produces grain. First the stalk comes up, then the head forms, and finally the full grain appears in the head. As soon as the grain ripens, the farmer brings it in, because the harvest is ready."

Then Jesus asked, "What can we say the kingdom of God is like? What story can we use to explain it? It's like a mustard seed, which is the smallest of all seeds on earth. But when it's planted, it grows and becomes the largest of all garden plants. Its branches are so big that birds can rest in its shade." Mark 4:26-32

Then Jesus left the crowd and went into the house. His disciples came to him and asked, "Please explain the story of the weeds in the field to us."

He replied, "The one who planted the good seed is the Son of Man. The field is the world, and the good seed stands for the people who belong to the kingdom. The weeds are the people who belong to the evil one, and the enemy who plants them is the devil. The harvest is the judgment day and the workers are angels.

"The weeds are pulled up and burned in the fire. That's how it will be on judgment day. The Son of Man will send out his angels, and they will weed out of his kingdom everything that causes sin and everyone who does wrong. They'll throw them into the blazing furnace, where people will weep and grind their teeth. Then God's people will shine like the sun in their Father's kingdom. Whoever understands should take this to heart.

"The kingdom of heaven is like treasure that was hidden in a field. When a man found it, he hid it again, and then he went and gladly sold everything he had to buy that field.

"Again, the kingdom of heaven is like a trader who was looking for fine pearls. When he found one that was very valuable, he went away and sold everything he had so he could buy that pearl.

"Again, the kingdom of heaven is like a net that was let down into the lake. It caught all kinds of fish. When it was full, the fishermen pulled it up onto the shore. Then they sat down and gathered the good fish into baskets, but they threw the bad fish away. That's how it will be on judgment day. The angels will come and separate the people who did wrong from those who did right. They will throw the bad people into the blazing furnace, where they will weep and grind their teeth.

"Do you understand all these things?" Jesus asked.

"Yes," they replied.

He said to them, "Every teacher of the law who has become a disciple in the kingdom of heaven is like the owner of a house who brings new treasures out of his storeroom along with the old ones." Matt. 13:36-52

Jesus spoke the message to them using many stories like these, telling them as much as they could understand. He didn't teach them anything without using a story. But when he was alone with his disciples, he explained everything to them. Mark 4:33-34

CHAPTER 8

CALMING A STORM

One day Jesus said to his disciples, "Let's go over to the other side of the lake." So they got into a boat and headed out. As they were sailing, Jesus fell asleep. Then a storm came down on the lake. It was so severe that the boat was about to sink, so they were all in great danger.

The disciples went and woke Jesus up, saying, "Master! Master! We're going to drown!"

But he got up and ordered the wind and the huge waves to stop raging. The storm quieted down, and everything became completely calm. "Where is your faith?" he asked his disciples.

They were amazed and filled with fear. They asked one another, "Who is this? He even commands the winds and the waves, and they obey him." Luke 8:22-25

They went across the Sea of Galilee to the area of the Gerasenes. When Jesus got out of the boat, a man controlled by an evil spirit came out of the tombs to meet him. He lived in the tombs, and no one could keep him tied up anymore, not even with a chain. His hands and feet had often been chained, but he tore the chains apart and broke the iron cuffs off his ankles. No one was strong enough to control him. Night and day, among the tombs and in the hills, he screamed and cut himself with stones.

When he saw Jesus from a distance, he ran to him and fell on his knees in front of him. He shouted at the top of his voice, "Jesus, Son of the Most High God, what do you want with me? Swear by God that you won't hurt me!" This was because Jesus had already said, "Come out of this man, you evil spirit!"

Then Jesus asked the demon, "What is your name?"

"My name is Legion," he answered, "because there are many of us." He begged Jesus again and again not to send them out of the area.

A large herd of pigs was feeding on a hillside nearby. The demons begged Jesus, "Send us among the pigs. Let us go into them." Jesus permitted that, and the evil spirits came out of the man and went into the pigs. There were about 2,000 pigs in the herd. They all rushed down the steep bank, ran into the lake, and drowned.

Those who were tending the pigs ran off and told the people in the town and countryside what had happened. The people went out to see for themselves. When they got to Jesus, they found the man who'd been controlled by many demons sitting there quietly. He was now dressed and thinking clearly. All this made the people afraid. Those who'd been there told them what had happened to the man and to the pigs. The people asked Jesus to leave their region.

As Jesus was getting into the boat, the man who'd been controlled by the demons begged to go with him, but Jesus wouldn't let him. Instead, he said, "Go home to your own people and tell them how much the Lord has done for you and how kind he has been to you."

So the man went to the area known as the Ten Cities and began telling how much Jesus had done for him. And all the people were amazed.

Jesus went by boat back across the Sea of Galilee. When he landed on the other side, a large crowd gathered around him. A man named Jairus, who was a synagogue leader, came with the crowd. When he saw Jesus, he bowed down to the ground in front of him and begged him, "My little daughter is dying. Please come and place your hands on her to heal her, and then she'll live."

So Jesus went with him. A large group of people came along with them, and they were crowding all around Jesus. Among them was a woman who had a sickness that made her bleed. She'd had it for 12 years and she'd suffered a great deal, even though she'd gone to many doctors. Though she'd spent all the money she had, she didn't get better. She kept getting worse!

But then she heard about Jesus, and she thought, "If I just touch his clothes, I'll be healed." So she came up behind him in the crowd and touched his clothes. Right away her bleeding stopped. She felt in her body that she was free from her suffering.

Jesus knew right away that some power had gone out from him. He turned around in the crowd and asked, "Who touched my clothes?"

"You can see all these people crowding around you," his disciples responded. "So why are you asking, 'Who touched me?' "

But Jesus kept looking around to see who had touched him. Then the woman came and fell at his feet. She knew what had happened to her, and she was shaking with fear, but she told him the whole truth. He said to her, "My daughter, your faith has healed you. Go in peace and be freed from your suffering."

While Jesus was still speaking, some people came from the house of Jairus, the synagogue leader. "Your daughter is dead," they told him. "Why bother the teacher anymore?"

Jesus heard what they were saying. He told Jairus, "Don't be afraid. Just believe."

Jesus only let Peter, James, and John, the brother of James, come with him. As they approached the home of the synagogue leader, they could hear the noise of people crying and sobbing loudly. Jesus went inside and asked them, "Why are you all crying so loudly? The child isn't dead. She's only sleeping." But they laughed at him.

He made them all go outside, and he brought only the child's father and mother and his disciples in to where the child was. He took her by the hand and said to her, *"Talitha koum!"* (That means, "Little girl, I say to you, get up!")

Right away the girl, who was 12 years old, stood up and began to walk around. They were totally amazed at this. Jesus gave them strict orders not to let anyone know what had happened, and he told them to give her something to eat. Mark 5:1-43

As Jesus went on from there, two blind men followed him. They called out, "Have mercy on us, Son of David!"

Jesus went indoors, and the blind men came to him. He asked them, "Do you believe that I can do this?"

"Yes, Lord," they replied.

Then he touched their eyes and said, "May it happen to you just as you have believed."

Then they could see. Jesus warned them sternly, "Make sure that no one knows about this." But they went out and spread the news about him all over that area. Matt. 9:27-31

Jesus left there and went to his hometown of Nazareth. His disciples came with him. On the Sabbath day, he began to teach in the synagogue.

Many who heard him were amazed. "Where did this man get these things?" they asked. "What's this wisdom that has been given to him? What are these remarkable miracles that he's doing? Isn't this the carpenter? Isn't he Mary's son? Isn't he the brother of James, Joseph, Judas, and Simon? And aren't his sisters here with us?"

They didn't think he really was who he seemed to be.

Jesus told them, "A prophet is honored everywhere except in his own town, among his relatives and in his own home."

He couldn't do any miracles there except place his hands on a few sick people and heal them. He was amazed at their lack of faith. Mark 6:1-6

Jesus went through all the towns and villages, teaching in their synagogues, preaching the good news of the kingdom, and healing every illness and sickness. When he saw the crowds, he felt deep concern for them, because they looked ragged and bewildered, like sheep without a shepherd. Then Jesus said to his disciples, "The harvest is great, but there are only a few workers. Ask the Lord of the harvest to send workers out into his harvest field." Matt. 9:35-38

Jesus called together the 12 disciples and gave them power and authority to drive out all demons and to heal sicknesses. Then he sent them out to announce God's kingdom and heal those who were sick. Luke 9:1-2

Jesus sent the 12 out with the following orders: "Don't go among the Gentiles and don't enter any town where the Samaritans live. Instead, go to the lost sheep of Israel. As you go, preach this message: 'The kingdom of heaven is near.' Heal the sick, bring the dead back to life, make those who have skin diseases clean again, and drive out demons. You have received freely, so give freely.

"Don't take any gold, silver, or copper coins with you in your belts. Don't bring a bag for the journey, or any extra clothes or sandals or a walking stick. A worker deserves to be given what's needed. When you enter a town or village, look for a person who's willing to welcome you, and stay at their house until you leave. As you enter their home, give it your blessing of peace. If the home deserves it, your peace will rest upon it; if it doesn't deserve it, your peace will return to you. Some people may not welcome you or listen to your words. If they don't, leave that home or town and shake the dust off your feet. Truly I tell you, on judgment day it will be easier for Sodom and Gomorrah than for that town.

"I'm sending you out like sheep among wolves. So be as wise as snakes and as harmless as doves. Be careful who you trust! You'll be turned over to the local courts and whipped in the synagogues. You'll be put on trial before governors and kings because of me, as witnesses to them and to the Gentiles. But when they arrest you, don't worry about what you'll say or how to say it. You'll be given the right words at the time. It won't even be you speaking. The Spirit of your Father will be speaking through you.

"Brothers will betray brothers to those who want to kill them, and fathers will betray their children. Children will rebel against their parents and have them put to death. Everyone will hate you because of me. But anyone who stands firm to the end will be saved. If people attack you in one place, escape to another. Truly I tell you, you won't finish going through the towns of Israel before the Son of Man comes.

"The student isn't greater than the teacher, and the slave isn't greater than the master. It's enough for students to be like their teachers and for slaves to be like their masters. If the head of the household has been called Beelzebul, the prince of demons, what should the others who live in the house expect to be called?

"Don't be afraid of your enemies. Everything that's now secret will be brought out into the open and everything that's hidden will be revealed. Repeat in the daylight what I tell you in the dark, and shout from the rooftops what is whispered in your ear. Don't be afraid of those who kill the body but can't kill the soul. Instead, be afraid of the one who can destroy both soul and body in hell. Aren't two sparrows sold for only a penny? But not one of them falls to the ground without your Father being aware of it. He even knows every hair on your head! So don't be afraid; you're worth more than many sparrows.

"If anyone tells others that they know me, I'll tell my Father in heaven that I know them. But if anyone denies that they know me, I'll tell my Father in heaven that I don't know them.

"Don't think that I've come to bring peace to the earth. I haven't come to bring peace, but a sword. I've come to turn " 'sons against their fathers, daughters against their mothers, and daughters-in-law against their mothers-in-law. A man's enemies will be the members of his own family.'

"Anyone who loves their father or mother more than me is not worthy of me. Anyone who loves their son or daughter more than me is not worthy of me. Whoever doesn't pick up their cross and follow me is not worthy of me. Whoever finds their life will lose it, but whoever loses their life because of me will find it.

"Anyone who welcomes you welcomes me, and anyone who welcomes me welcomes the one who sent me. If someone welcomes a prophet because they're a prophet, that person will receive a prophet's reward. If someone welcomes a godly person because they're godly, that person will receive a godly person's reward. And if someone even gives a cup of cold water to a little one who follows me, truly I tell you, that person will be rewarded." Matt. 10:5-42

King Herod heard about this because Jesus' name had become well known. Some were saying, "He's John the Baptist, raised from the dead! That's why he has the power to do miracles."

Others said, "He's Elijah!"

Still others claimed, "He's a prophet, like those of long ago."

But when Herod heard this, he said, "I had John's head cut off, but now he has been raised from the dead!"

It was Herod himself who'd given the orders to arrest John. He had him tied up and put in prison because of Herodias, the woman who had been the wife of his brother Philip, but who was now married to him. John had been saying to Herod, "The Law of Moses doesn't permit you to be married to your brother's wife." Herodias had a grudge against John because he said that, and she wanted to kill him. But she wasn't able to, because Herod was afraid of John and kept him safe. Herod knew John was a holy man who did what was right. When he listened to him, he always felt uncomfortable, but he still liked to hear John speak.

Herodias got her opportunity when Herod gave a banquet on his birthday. He invited his high officials, his military commanders, and the most important leaders of Galilee. The daughter of Herodias came in and danced for Herod and his dinner guests, and they were all very pleased.

The king told the girl, "Ask me for anything you want, and I'll give it to you." He made this promise in front of everyone. "I'll give you anything you ask for," he insisted, "even up to half of my kingdom."

She went out to her mother and said, "What should I ask for?"

She answered, "The head of John the Baptist."

The girl hurried back to the king and said, "I want you to give me the head of John the Baptist on a platter, right now."

The king was very upset. But because he'd made a promise in front of all his dinner guests, he didn't want to say no to the girl. So right away he sent a man out with orders to bring John's head. The man went to the prison and cut John's head off, and then he brought it back on a platter. He gave it to the girl, and she gave it to her mother.

When John's disciples heard about this, they came and took his body and placed it in a tomb. Mark 6:14-29

CHAPTER 9

FEEDING THE HUNGRY CROWDS

The apostles gathered around Jesus and told him everything they'd done and taught. So many people were coming and going around them that they didn't even have a chance to eat. So Jesus told them, "I want you to come with me to a quiet place where you can get some rest."

So they headed off by themselves in a boat to a quiet place. But many people saw them leaving and recognized who they were. People ran from all the towns to where they were heading, and they got there ahead of them. When Jesus came ashore, he found a large crowd. He felt deep concern for them because they were like sheep without a shepherd. So he began to teach them many things. Mark 6:30-34

When it was almost evening, the disciples came to him. "We're in the middle of nowhere," they told him, "and it's already getting late. Send the crowds away so they can go to the villages and buy some food."

Jesus answered, "They don't need to go away. You give them something to eat." Matt. 14:15-16

When Jesus looked up and saw a large crowd coming toward him, he said to Philip, "Where can we buy bread for all these people to eat?" He asked this only to challenge Philip. He already knew what he was going to do.

Philip answered, "We'd have to spend more than half a year's pay to buy enough bread for each person to have just a bite!"

Another of his disciples spoke up. It was Andrew, Simon Peter's brother. He said, "There's a boy here who has five small loaves of barley bread and a couple of small fish. But how far will that go to feed such a large crowd?"

Jesus said, "Have the people sit down." There was plenty of grass for everyone to sit on. Only counting the men, there were about 5,000 in the crowd.

Jesus took the loaves and gave thanks, and then they were distributed to the people where they sat. He did the same with the fish. They gave out as much as each person wanted.

When everyone had enough to eat, Jesus told his disciples, "Collect the leftover pieces. Let's not waste anything." So they picked up the leftovers and filled 12 baskets with the extra pieces. That's how much was still left from the five barley loaves after everyone had eaten.

When the people saw the sign that Jesus had done, they began to say, "This must be the Prophet who was supposed to come into the world!" John 6:5-14

Afterwards Jesus made the disciples get right into the boat and go on ahead of him to the other side of the lake while he said goodbye to the crowd. Once the crowd was gone, he went up on a mountainside by himself to pray.

Later that night, he was still up there alone. Then the boat the disciples were in was a long way from land. It started being pounded by the waves, because the wind was blowing against it.

Shortly before dawn, Jesus went out to the disciples, walking on the lake. When they saw him walking on the lake, they were terrified. "It's a ghost!" they exclaimed, crying out in fear.

But Jesus called out to them right away, "Don't worry; it's me! Don't be afraid."

"If it's really you, Lord," Peter said, "tell me to come to you on the water."

"Come," Jesus said.

So Peter got out of the boat and walked on the water toward Jesus. But when Peter saw the power of the wind, he got frightened and began to sink. "Lord!" he cried out, "save me!"

Jesus reached right out with his hand and caught him. "You have such little faith!" he said. "Why did you doubt?"

When they climbed into the boat, the wind died down. Then those in the boat worshiped Jesus, saying, "You're the Son of God!"

They crossed over the lake and landed at Gennesaret. The people who lived there recognized Jesus and sent word all over the nearby countryside. They brought all the sick to Jesus and begged him to let them just touch a tassel on his clothes. Everyone who did so was healed. Matt. 14:22-36

The next day the crowd that had stayed on the other side of the lake started to wonder where Jesus was. They knew that only one boat had been there and that Jesus hadn't gotten into it with his disciples. Then some boats arrived from Tiberias, near the place where the people had eaten the bread after the Lord gave thanks, and the crowd realized that Jesus and his disciples weren't there. So they got into boats and went to Capernaum to look for Jesus.

They found him on the other side of the lake and asked him, "Rabbi, when did you come here?"

Jesus answered, "Truly I tell you, you're not looking for me because you saw the signs I did. You're looking for me because you ate as much bread as you wanted. Don't work for food that spoils, but for food that lasts forever. Work for the food that the Son of Man will give you, because God the Father has put his seal of approval on him."

Then they asked him, "What works does God want us to do?"

Jesus answered, "God's work is to believe in the one he has sent."

So they asked him, "Then what sign will you give us so we can see it and believe you? Long ago our people ate the manna in the desert. It is written in Scripture, 'The Lord gave them bread from heaven to eat.' "

Jesus said to them, "Truly I tell you, it isn't Moses who has given you the bread from heaven, it's my Father who gives you the true bread from heaven. The bread of God is the bread that comes down from heaven and gives life to the world."

"Sir," they said, "give us this bread all the time."

Then Jesus said, "I am the bread of life. Whoever comes to me will never go hungry. Whoever believes in me will never be thirsty. But it's just as I told you—you've seen me, but you still don't believe. Everyone the Father gives me will come to me, and I'll never turn any of them away. I haven't come down from heaven to do my own will; I've come to do the will of the one who sent me. And the one who sent me doesn't want me to lose any of those he has given me. He wants me to raise them up on the last day. My Father wants everyone who looks to the Son and believes in him to have eternal life. And I will raise them up on the last day."

Then the Jews there began to complain about Jesus because he'd said, "I am the bread that came down from heaven." They asked, "Isn't this Jesus—Joseph's son? We know who his father and mother are. So how can he now claim, 'I came down from heaven'?"

"Stop grumbling," Jesus told them. "No one can come to me unless the Father who sent me attracts them. Then I will raise them up on the last day. It's written in the Prophets, 'God will teach all of them.' Everyone who has heard the Father and learned from him comes to me. No one has seen the Father except the one who has come from God. Only he has seen the Father. Truly I tell you, everyone who believes has eternal life. I am the bread of life. Long ago your people ate the manna in the desert, and they still died. But the bread that comes down from heaven is here. Anyone can eat it and not die. I am the living bread that came down from heaven. Whoever eats of this bread will live forever. This bread is my flesh, which I will give for the life of the world."

Then the Jews began to argue sharply among themselves, asking, "How can this man give us his flesh to eat?"

Jesus said to them, "Truly I tell you, unless you eat the Son of Man's flesh and drink his blood, you don't have any life in you. Whoever eats my flesh and drinks my blood has eternal life, and I will raise them up on the last day, because my flesh is real food and my blood is real drink. Whoever eats my flesh and drinks my blood remains in me and I remain in them. Just as the living Father sent me and I live because of him, so those who feed on me will live because of me. This is the bread that came down from heaven. Long ago your people ate manna and died, but whoever eats this bread will live forever."

He said this while he was teaching in the synagogue in Capernaum. Many of Jesus' disciples said when they heard this, "This is an unpleasant message. Who can accept it?"

Jesus knew that his disciples were complaining about this message. So he said to them, "Does this offend you? Then what if you see the Son of Man go back up to where he was before? The Spirit gives life; the flesh isn't worth anything. The words I've spoken to you are full of the Spirit and they give life. But there are some of you who don't believe." Jesus had known from the beginning which of them did not believe and who was going to hand him over to his enemies. He went on to say, "That's why I told you that no one can come to me unless the Father grants that."

From this time on, many of his disciples turned back and no longer followed him.

Jesus asked the 12 disciples, "You don't want to leave too, do you?"

Simon Peter answered, "Lord, where would we go to? You have the words of eternal life. We have come to believe and to know that you are the Holy One of God."

Then Jesus replied, "Haven't I chosen you 12 disciples? But one of you is a devil!" He meant Judas Iscariot, one of the 12 disciples, who was later going to hand Jesus over to his enemies. John 6:22-71

The Pharisees and some of the teachers of the law who'd come from Jerusalem gathered around Jesus. They saw some of his disciples eating food with hands that were unclean, that is, not ceremonially washed. The Pharisees and all the Jews never eat until they've washed their hands to make them clean. Their elders teach that they have to do that. When they come home from the market, they have to take a bath before they can eat anything. And they follow many other teachings too. For example, they wash cups, pitchers, and kettles in a special way.

So the Pharisees and the teachers of the law asked Jesus, "Why don't your disciples follow what the elders teach? Why do they eat their food with unclean hands?"

Jesus answered, "Isaiah was right when he prophesied about you hypocrites! He said, " 'These people honor me by what they say, but their hearts are far away from me. Their worship doesn't mean anything to me, because they're only teaching human rules.' You've let go of God's commands, and instead you're holding on to teachings that people have passed down."

Jesus continued, "You have a fine way of setting aside God's commands so that you can follow your own teachings. Moses said, 'Honor your father and mother.' He also said, 'Anyone who curses their father or mother must be put to death.' But you tell people that if they have money that they could use to help their parents, they can say instead that it's Corban. (That means 'a gift set apart for God.') So you no longer allow them to do anything for their parents anymore. You make the word of God useless by putting your own teachings in its place. And you do this a lot."

Jesus called the crowd to him again and said, "Listen to me, everyone, and understand this. Nothing that's outside of a person can make them unclean by going into them. It's what comes out of a person that makes them unclean." Mark 7:1-16

Then the disciples came to him and said, "Did you know that the Pharisees got angry when they heard that?"

Jesus replied, "Every plant that my heavenly Father hasn't planted will be pulled up by the roots. Don't worry about the Pharisees. They're blind guides. If one blind person leads another, they'll both fall into a pit."

Peter asked, "But what did you mean by what you said?"

"Don't you understand yet?" Jesus replied. "Don't you see? Everything that enters the mouth goes into the stomach, and from there it goes out of the body. But the things that come out of a person's mouth come from the heart. Those are the things that make someone unclean. Out of a person's heart come cruel thoughts, murder, adultery, other sexual sins, stealing, false testimony, and lies. Those are the things that make you unclean. But eating without washing your hands doesn't make you unclean."

Jesus left Galilee and went to the area of Tyre and Sidon. A Canaanite woman who lived near there came to him and cried out, "Lord! Son of David! Have mercy on me! A demon has been controlling my daughter and making her suffer terribly."

Jesus didn't say a word. So his disciples came and begged him, "Tell her to go away! She keeps following us and crying out for help."

Jesus answered, "I was sent only to the lost sheep of Israel."

Then the woman fell on her knees in front of him. "Lord! Help me!" she said.

He replied, "It's not right to take the children's bread and throw it out to the dogs."

"That's true, Lord," she said, "but even the dogs eat the crumbs that fall from their owner's table."

Then Jesus said to her, "Woman, you have great faith! You will receive what you've asked for." And her daughter was healed at that moment. Matt. 15:12-28

Then Jesus left the area of Tyre and went through Sidon, down to the Sea of Galilee, and into the area known as the Ten Cities. There some people brought a man to Jesus who was deaf and could hardly speak. They begged Jesus to place his hands on the man.

Jesus took the man to one side, away from the crowd. He put his fingers into the man's ears, and then he spit and touched the man's tongue. Jesus looked up to heaven and said to the man with a deep sigh, "*Ephphatha!*" which means, "Be opened!"

The man's ears were opened, his tongue was freed up, and he began to speak clearly. Jesus ordered the people not to tell anyone. But the more he did, the more they kept talking about it. People were overwhelmed and amazed and said, "He has done everything well. He even makes deaf people able to hear, and he makes those who can't speak able to talk." Mark 7:31-37

Then Jesus called his disciples to him and said, "I'm concerned for these people because they've already been with me for three days and they've run out of food to eat. I don't want to send them away hungry, because if I do, they may be too weak to make it back home."

His disciples answered, "Where could we get enough bread to feed this large crowd? We're in the middle of nowhere."

"How many loaves do you have?" Jesus asked.

"Seven," they replied, "and a few small fish."

Jesus told the crowd to sit down on the ground. Then he took the seven loaves and the fish, gave thanks, broke them, and gave them to the disciples. They passed them out to the people. Everyone ate as much as they wanted, and after that, the disciples picked up seven full baskets of leftover pieces. Just counting the men, they fed about 4,000 people, and there were many women and children as well.

Jesus sent the crowd away, and then he got into the boat and went to the area near Magadan. Matt. 15:32-39

They crossed over to the other side of the lake, but the disciples forgot to bring bread.

"Be careful," Jesus said to them. "Watch out for the yeast of the Pharisees and Sadducees."

The disciples talked this over among themselves and decided, "He must be saying this because we didn't bring any bread."

Jesus knew what they were saying, and he responded, "How little faith you have! Why are you talking to each other about not having any bread? Don't you understand yet? Don't you remember the five loaves that fed the 5,000, and how many full baskets of leftover pieces you picked up? Don't you remember the seven loaves that fed the 4,000, and how many full baskets of leftover pieces you picked up? How can you possibly not understand? I wasn't talking to you about bread. I was telling you to watch out for the yeast of the Pharisees and Sadducees."

Then the disciples understood that Jesus wasn't telling them to watch out for the yeast that's used in bread. He was warning them against the teaching of the Pharisees and Sadducees. Matt. 16:5-12

CHAPTER 10

SEEN IN GOD'S GLORY

Jesus came with his disciples to Bethsaida, and there some people brought a blind man to Jesus and begged him to touch him. He took him by the hand and led him outside the village. Then he spit on the man's eyes and placed his hands on him. "Do you see anything?" Jesus asked.

The man looked up and said, "I see people, but they look like trees walking around."

Jesus put his hands on the man's eyes again, and when he opened his eyes wide, his sight was restored, and he could see everything clearly. Jesus sent him straight home, telling him, "Don't even go into the village."

Jesus and his disciples went on to the villages around Caesarea Philippi. On the way he asked them, "Who do people say I am?"

They answered, "Some say John the Baptist, others say Elijah, and others say one of the prophets." Mark 8:22-28

"But what about you?" he asked. "Who do you say I am?"

Simon Peter answered, "You are the Messiah, the Son of the living God."

Jesus replied, "Blessed are you, Simon, son of Jonah! No mere human showed that to you, but my Father in heaven. I tell you that you are Peter, and on this rock, I will build my church. The gates of Hades won't be too strong for it. I'll give you the keys to the kingdom of heaven, so that what you lock on earth will be locked in heaven and what you unlock on earth will be unlocked in heaven."

Then Jesus ordered his disciples not to tell anyone he was the Messiah. From that time on Jesus began to explain to his disciples what would happen to him. He told them he would have to go to Jerusalem and that the elders, chief priests, and teachers of the law would make him suffer many things there. He would be killed, but he would rise again on the third day.

Peter took Jesus to one side and began to berate him. "Never, Lord!" he said. "That will never happen to you!"

Jesus turned and said to Peter, "Get behind me, Satan! You're like a rock in my path to trip me. You're not thinking about what God wants. You're only thinking about what people want."

Then Jesus told his disciples, "All those who want to be my disciples must say 'no' to themselves, pick up their crosses, and follow me. Whoever wants to save their life will lose it, but whoever loses their life for me will find it. What good is it if someone gains the whole world but loses their soul? What can anyone trade for their soul? The Son of Man is going to come with his angels in his Father's glory, and he will deal with each person according to what they've done. "Truly I tell you, some who are standing here right now will not die before they see the Son of Man coming in his kingdom." Matt. 16:15-28

About eight days after Jesus had said this, he took Peter, John, and James with him and went up on a mountain to pray. As he was praying, the appearance of his face changed, and his clothes became as bright as a flash of lightning. Two men, Moses and Elijah, appeared in shining glory.

Jesus and the two of them talked together about how he would be leaving soon and how this was going to happen in Jerusalem. Peter and his companions were very sleepy, but becoming fully awake, they saw Jesus' glory and the two men standing with him. Luke 9:28-32

Peter said to Jesus, "Lord, it's good for us to be here. If you'd like, I can set up three shelters—one for you, one for Moses, and one for Elijah."

While Peter was still speaking, a bright cloud covered them. A voice from the cloud said, "This is my beloved Son, and I'm very pleased with him. Listen to him!"

When the disciples heard this, they were terrified and fell with their faces to the ground. But Jesus came and touched them. "Get up," he said, "don't be afraid." When they looked up, no one was there except Jesus.

On the way down the mountain, Jesus told them, "Don't tell anyone what you've seen until the Son of Man has been raised from the dead."

The disciples asked him, "Why do the teachers of the law say that Elijah has to come first?"

Jesus replied, "Elijah is supposed to come and put everything back in order. But I tell you, Elijah has already come. But people didn't recognize him, so they did whatever they wanted to him. In the same way, they're going to make the Son of Man suffer."

Then the disciples understood that Jesus was talking to them about John the Baptist. Matt. 17:4-13

When they got back to the other disciples, they found a large crowd standing around them, and the teachers of the law were arguing with them. When all the people saw Jesus, they were filled with wonder and they ran to greet him.

"What are you arguing about with them?" Jesus asked.

A man in the crowd answered, "Teacher, I brought my son to you. He's controlled by an evil spirit that keeps him from speaking. Whenever it takes hold of him, it throws him to the ground. He foams at the mouth and grinds his teeth, and his body becomes stiff. I asked your disciples to drive out the spirit, but they couldn't."

"You unbelieving generation!" Jesus responded. "How long am I going to be with you? How long do I have to put up with you? Bring the boy to me."

So they brought him. As soon as the spirit saw Jesus, it threw the boy into a fit. He fell to the ground and rolled around, foaming at the mouth.

Jesus asked the boy's father, "How long has he been like this?"

"Since he was a child," he answered. "The spirit has often thrown him into the fire or into the water to try to kill him. But if you can do anything, take pity on us and help us."

" 'If you can'?" asked Jesus. "Everything is possible for someone who believes!"

"I do believe!" the boy's father cried out. "Help me overcome my unbelief!"

When Jesus saw that a crowd was running over to see what was happening, he ordered the evil spirit to leave the boy. "You spirit that makes him unable to hear and speak," he said, "I command you, come out of him and never enter him again."

The spirit screamed and shook the boy wildly, then it came out of him. The boy looked so lifeless that many people said, "He's dead." But Jesus took him by the hand and lifted him to his feet, and he stood up.

After Jesus had gone indoors, his disciples asked him privately, "Why couldn't we drive out the evil spirit?"

He replied, "This kind can come out only by prayer."

They left that place and went through Galilee. Jesus didn't want anyone to know where they were, because he was instructing his disciples. He said to them, "The Son of Man is going to be handed over to people who will kill him, but after three days he will rise from the dead."

But they didn't understand what he meant, and they were afraid to ask him about it. Mark 9:14-32

Jesus and his disciples arrived in Capernaum. There the people who collected the temple tax came to Peter and asked him, "Does your teacher pay the temple tax?"

"Yes, he does," he replied.

When Peter came into the house, Jesus spoke to him first. "What do you think, Simon?" he asked. "Who do the kings of the earth collect taxes and fees from? Do they collect them from their own children, or from others?"

"From others," Peter answered.

"Then the children don't have to pay," Jesus responded. "But let's not put an obstacle in anyone's way. Go to the lake and throw out your fishing line. Open the mouth of first fish you catch, and you'll find a coin that's the exact amount you need. Take it and give it to them for my tax and yours." Matt. 17:24-27

At that time the disciples came to Jesus and asked him, "Who is the greatest in the kingdom of heaven?"

Jesus called a little child over and had them stand in the middle of the group. Jesus then said, "Truly I tell you, unless you change and become like little children, you'll never enter the kingdom of heaven. Whoever becomes humble like this little child is the greatest in the kingdom of heaven. And anyone who welcomes a child like this one in my name welcomes me.

"But what if someone causes one of these little ones who believe in me to sin? It would be better for them to be thrown into the sea with a large millstone hung around their neck and drown at the bottom. Woe to the world because of the things that cause people to sin! Things like that must come. Woe to the person who causes them! If your hand or foot causes you to sin, cut it off and throw it away. It's better to enter life with only one hand or foot than to go with two hands or two feet into hell, where the fire burns forever. If your eye causes you to sin, pull it out and throw it away. It's better to enter life with one eye than to be thrown into the fire of hell with two eyes.

"Make sure you don't look down on one of these little ones. I tell you, their angels in heaven see face to face my Father who is in heaven." Matt. 18:1-11

"Teacher," John said, "we saw someone driving out demons in your name, and we told him to stop because he wasn't one of us."

"Don't stop him," Jesus said. "No one who does a miracle in my name can say anything bad about me right afterwards. Anyone who isn't against us is for us. Truly I tell you, anyone who gives you a cup of water in my name because you belong to the Messiah will certainly receive a reward. Mark 9:38-41

"If your brother or sister sins against you, go and tell them privately what they've done wrong. If they listen to you, you've won them back. But if they won't listen to you, return with one or two others. Scripture says, 'Every matter must be proved by the words of two or three witnesses.' If they still refuse to listen, then tell it to the community of believers. And if they refuse to listen even to the community, then treat them the way you would treat an unbeliever or a traitor.

"Truly I tell you, what you tie up on earth will be tied up in heaven, and what you set free on earth will be set free in heaven.

"Again, I tell you truly, if two of you on earth agree about anything you ask for, my Father in heaven will do it for you. Where two or three people gather in my name, I am there with them."

Peter came to Jesus and asked, "Lord, how many times should I forgive a brother or sister who sins against me? Up to seven times?"

Jesus answered, "Not seven times, I tell you, but 77 times.

"The kingdom of heaven is like a king who wanted to collect all the money his servants owed him. First, they brought him a man who owed 10,000 bags of gold. Since he wasn't able to pay, his master ordered the man, his wife, his children, and everything he owned to be sold to pay back the debt.

"Then the servant got down on his knees in front of him. 'Give me time,' he begged, 'and I'll pay everything back.' His master felt sorry for him, so he forgave him what he owed and let him go.

"But then that servant went out and found another servant, who owed him 100 silver coins. He grabbed him and began to choke him. 'Pay back what you owe me!' he demanded.

"The other servant got down on his knees. 'Give me time,' he begged him, 'and I'll pay it back.'

"But the first servant refused. Instead, he went and had the man thrown into prison until he paid back what he owed. When the other servants saw this, it made them very angry. They went and told their master everything that had happened.

"Then the master called the first servant back in. 'You ungrateful servant,' he said. 'I forgave you everything you owed because you begged me to. Shouldn't you have had mercy on the other servant, just as I had mercy on you?' The master was so angry that handed him over to the jailers to be punished until he paid back everything he owed.

"That's how my Father in heaven will treat each of you if you don't forgive your brother or sister from your heart." Matt. 18:15-35

CHAPTER 11

CLAIMING GOD'S NAME

After this, Jesus traveled around in Galilee. He didn't want to travel around in Judea because the Jewish leaders there were looking for a way to kill him. But when it was almost time for the Jewish Feast of Shelters, Jesus' brothers told him, "Leave Galilee and go to Judea. That way your disciples there will be able to see the works that you do. No one who wants to be well known does things in secret. Since you're doing these things, show yourself to the world."

Even Jesus' own brothers did not believe in him. So Jesus told them, "My time hasn't come yet. For you, any time would be the right time. The people of the world can't hate you, but they hate me because I'm a witness that what they're doing is wrong. You go to the feast. I'm not going up to this feast because my time hasn't yet fully come."

After saying that, he stayed in Galilee. However, after his brothers had left for the feast, he went too. But he went secretly, not openly. John 7:1-10

When the time grew near for Jesus to be taken up to heaven, he resolved to go to Jerusalem. He sent messengers on ahead, and they went into a Samaritan village to get things ready for him. But the people there wouldn't welcome Jesus, because he was heading for Jerusalem.

The disciples James and John saw this and asked, "Lord, do you want us to call down fire from heaven to destroy them?"

But Jesus turned and commanded them not to. Then he and his disciples headed off to another village.

As they continued down the road, a man said to Jesus, "I will follow you no matter where you go."

Jesus answered, "Foxes have dens and birds have nests, but the Son of Man has no place to lay his head."

He said to another man, "Follow me."

But that man replied, "Lord, first let me go and bury my father."

Jesus said to him, "Let those who are dead bury their own dead; you go and tell others about God's kingdom."

Still another person said, "I will follow you, Lord, but first let me go back and say goodbye to my family."

Jesus responded, "Anyone who starts to plow but then looks back isn't fit for service in God's kingdom." Luke 9:51-62

At the feast, the Jewish leaders were watching for Jesus. They were asking, "Where is he?"

Many people in the crowd were whispering about him. Some said, "He's a good man."

Others replied, "No, he's misleading the people." But no one would say anything about him openly because they were afraid of the leaders.

When the feast was halfway over, Jesus went up to the temple courtyard and began to teach. The Jews there were amazed and asked, "How can this man know so much when he's never been taught?"

Jesus answered, "What I'm teaching doesn't come from me, but from the one who sent me. If anyone chooses to do God's will, they'll know whether my teaching comes from God or from me. Whoever speaks on their own does it to get personal glory, but anyone who works for the glory of the one who sent him can be trusted. There's nothing dishonest about him. Didn't Moses give you the law? But not one of you obeys the law. Why are you trying to kill me?"

"You're controlled by a demon!" the crowd answered. "Who's trying to kill you?"

Jesus said to them, "I did a single miracle, and you're all amazed. Moses gave you the law about circumcision, and Abraham, Isaac, and Jacob had the custom even before that. So you circumcise a child on the Sabbath day. If you'll circumcise a boy on the Sabbath day so that you don't break the law of Moses, why are you angry with me? I healed a man's entire body on the Sabbath day! Stop judging only by what you see. Judge in the right way."

At that point some of the people of Jerusalem began to ask, "Isn't this the man they're trying to kill? Here he is, speaking in public, and they're not saying a word to him. Have the authorities really decided that he's the Messiah? But we know where this man is from. When the Messiah comes, no one will know where he's from."

Then Jesus, still teaching in the temple courtyard, cried out, "Yes, you know me, and you know where I'm from. I'm not here on my own authority. The one who sent me is true. You don't know him, but I know him because I came from him and he sent me."

When he said this, they tried to arrest him. But no one laid a hand on him because his time hadn't come yet. Still, many people in the crowd believed in him. They asked, "When the Messiah comes, will he do more signs than this man?"

The Pharisees heard the crowd whispering things like this about him. So the chief priests and the Pharisees sent temple guards to arrest him.

Jesus told them, "I'm only going to be with you for a short time. Then I'll go to the one who sent me. You'll look for me, but you won't find me. You can't come where I am going."

The Jews asked each other, "Where is this man planning to go, if we won't be able to find him there? Will he go to where our people are living scattered among the Greeks, and will he teach the Greeks there? What did he mean when he said, 'You'll look for me, but you won't find me,' and 'You can't come where I am going'?"

On the last and most important day of the feast, Jesus stood up and called in a loud voice, "Let anyone who is thirsty come to me and drink! If anyone believes in me, rivers of living water will flow from inside them, just as Scripture says."

When he said this, he was referring to the Holy Spirit. Those who believed in Jesus would later receive the Spirit. But at that time, the Spirit had not been given, because Jesus hadn't been glorified yet.

When the people heard his words, some of them said, "This man must be the Prophet we've been expecting."

Others said, "He's the Messiah."

Still others asked, "How can the Messiah come from Galilee? Doesn't Scripture say that the Messiah will come from the family line of David and from Bethlehem, the town where David lived?" So the people didn't agree about who Jesus was. Some wanted to arrest him, but no one laid a hand on him.

Finally, the temple guards went back to the chief priests and the Pharisees, who asked them, "Why didn't you bring him in?"

"No one ever spoke the way this man does," the guards replied.

"You mean he has deceived you too?" the Pharisees asked. "Have any of the rulers or Pharisees believed in him? No! But God's curse is on this mob that knows nothing about the law."

Then Nicodemus, who had gone to Jesus earlier and who was one of the Pharisees, spoke up. He asked, "Does our law find a man guilty without listening to him first to find out what he has been doing?"

They answered, "Are you from Galilee too? Look into it—you'll find that no prophet is going to come out of Galilee."

Then they all went home. John 7:11-53

But Jesus went out to the Mount of Olives.

First thing in the morning, Jesus came back into the temple court-yard. All the people gathered around him there, and he sat down to teach them. The teachers of the law and the Pharisees brought in a woman who'd been caught committing adultery.

They made her stand in front of the group, and they said to Jesus, "Teacher, this woman was caught sleeping with a man who wasn't her husband. In the Law, Moses commanded us to kill women who commit adultery by throwing stones at them. But what do you say?"

They were trying to trap Jesus with that question, so they'd have a reason to bring charges against him.

But Jesus bent down and started to write on the ground with his finger. When they kept on asking him questions, he stood up and said to them, "If any of you has never sinned, he can be the first to throw a stone at her." He bent down again and wrote on the ground.

Those who heard what he had said began to go away one at a time. The older ones left first, and then the younger ones. Finally, only Jesus was left, with the woman still standing there.

Jesus stood up and asked her, "Woman, where are they? Has no one condemned you?"

"No one, sir," she said.

"Then I don't condemn you either," Jesus told her. "Go now and stop sinning."

Jesus spoke to the people again and said, "I am the light of the world. Anyone who follows me will never walk in darkness. They will have the light of life."

The Pharisees argued with him. "Here you are, appearing as your own witness," they complained. "What you say isn't valid."

Jesus answered, "Even if I am a witness about myself, what I say is valid. I know where I came from and where I'm going. But you have no idea where I come from or where I'm going. You judge by human standards; I don't judge anyone. But if I do judge, my decisions are right, because I'm not alone. I stand with the Father who sent me. Your own Law says that if two different people give the same evidence about something, their testimony can be trusted.

I'm a witness about myself, and the second witness about me is the Father who sent me."

Then they asked him, "Where is your father?"

"You don't know me or my Father," Jesus replied. "If you knew me, you would also know my Father."

He spoke these words while he was teaching in the temple courtyard near the place where the offerings were put. But no one arrested him, because his time hadn't come yet.

Once more Jesus said to them, "I'm going away. You will look for me, and you will die in your sin. You can't come where I'm going."

This made the Jews ask, "Is he going to kill himself? Is that why he's saying, 'You can't come where I'm going'?"

But Jesus continued, "You're from below; I'm from above. You're from this world; I'm not from this world. I told you that you would die in your sins. If you don't believe that I am he, you will certainly die in your sins."

"Who are you?" they asked.

"Just what I've been telling you from the beginning," Jesus replied. "I have much to say in judgment of you. But the one who sent me is trustworthy, and I'm telling the world what I've heard from him."

They didn't understand that Jesus was telling them about his Father. So Jesus said, "When you have lifted up the Son of Man, then you'll know that I am he. You'll also know that I don't do anything on my own. I speak just what the Father has taught me. The one who sent me is with me. He hasn't left me alone, because I always do what pleases him."

Even while Jesus was speaking, many people believed in him. Jesus said to the Jews who had believed him, "If you obey my teaching, you are really my disciples. Then you will know the truth, and the truth will set you free."

They answered him, "We're Abraham's children. We've never been slaves to anybody. So how can you say that we'll be set free?"

Jesus replied, "Truly I tell you, everyone who sins is a slave to sin. A slave has no lasting place in the family, but a son belongs to the family forever. So if the Son sets you free, you really will be free. I know that you're Abraham's children. But you're looking for a way to kill me, because you don't have any room for my word. I'm telling you what I saw when I was with my Father. You're doing what you've heard from your father."

"Abraham is our father," they answered.

"If you really were Abraham's children," Jesus said, "you would do what Abraham did. But you're looking for a way to kill me—a man who has told you the truth that I heard from God. Abraham didn't do the things you want to do. You're doing what your own father does."

"We know who our father is," they insisted. "The only Father we have is God himself."

Jesus said to them, "If God were your Father, you would love me, because I've come here from God. I haven't come on my own; God sent me. Why can't you understand what I'm saying? Because you can't really hear it. You belong to your father, the devil, and you want to carry out your father's wishes. From the beginning, the devil has been a murderer. He has never obeyed the truth because there's no truth in him. When he lies, he speaks his native language, because he is a liar and the father of lies. But because I tell the truth, you don't believe me! Can any of you prove that I'm guilty of sin? If I'm telling the truth, why don't you believe me? Whoever belongs to God hears what God says. The reason you don't hear is that you don't belong to God."

The Jews answered Jesus, "Aren't we right to say that you're a Samaritan and controlled by a demon?"

"I'm not controlled by a demon," Jesus replied. "I honor my Father, but you don't honor me. I'm not seeking glory for myself. But there is one who seeks it for me, and he is the judge. Truly I tell you, whoever obeys my word will never die."

At this they exclaimed, "Now we know you're controlled by a demon! Abraham died, and so did the prophets. But you're saying that whoever obeys your word will never die. Are you greater than our father Abraham? He died, and so did the prophets. Who do you think you are?"

Jesus answered, "If I bring glory to myself, my glory means nothing. My Father is the one who brings glory to me, and you claim him as your God. You don't know him, but I know him. If I said I didn't, I'd be a liar like you. But I do know him, and I obey his word. Your father Abraham was filled with joy at the thought of seeing my day. He saw it and was glad."

The Jews said to Jesus, "You're not even 50 years old, but you've seen Abraham?"

"Truly I tell you," Jesus answered, "before Abraham was born, *I Am.*"

When he said that, they picked up stones to kill him. But Jesus slipped out of sight and left the temple area. John 8:1-59

CHAPTER 12

WHO IS HE?

After this the Lord appointed 72 others and sent them out two by two ahead of him to every town and place where he was about to go.

The 72 returned with joy and said, "Lord, even the demons obey us when we speak in your name!"

Jesus answered, "I saw Satan fall like lightning from heaven. I've given you authority to stomp on snakes and scorpions, to destroy all the power of the enemy. Nothing will harm you. But don't be glad because the evil spirits obey you; instead, be glad that your names are written in heaven."

One day an expert in the law stood up to test Jesus. "Teacher," he asked, "what must I do to have eternal life?"

"What is written in the Law?" Jesus answered. "How do you understand it?"

He replied, " 'Love the Lord your God with all your heart, all your soul, all your strength, and all your mind,' and, 'Love your neighbor as you love yourself.' "

"You have answered correctly," Jesus replied. "Do that, and you will live."

But the man wanted to prove himself right, so he asked Jesus, "And who is my neighbor?"

Jesus responded, "A man was going down from Jerusalem to Jericho when robbers attacked him, stripped him of his clothes, and beat him. Then they went away, leaving him almost dead. A priest happened to be going down that same road, but when he saw the man, he passed by on the other side. A Levite also came by, and when he saw the man, he passed by on the other side too. But a Samaritan came to the place where the man was, and when he saw him, he felt compassion for him. He went over to him and poured olive oil and wine on his wounds and bandaged them. Then he put the man on his own donkey and brought him to an inn, and there he took care of him. The next day he took out two silver coins and gave them to the owner of the inn. 'Take care of this man,' he told him. 'When I return, I'll pay you for any extra expenses this doesn't cover.'

"Which of the three," Jesus asked, "do you think was a neighbor to the man who was attacked by the robbers?"

The expert in the law replied, "The one who took care of him."

Jesus told him, "Go and do as he did."

As Jesus was on his way with his disciples, he came to a certain village, and there a woman named Martha welcomed him into her home. She had a sister named Mary, who sat at the Lord's feet listening to what he said. Martha, meanwhile, was busy with all the entertaining. She came to Jesus and said, "Lord, don't you care that my sister has left me to do the work all by myself? Tell her to help me!"

"Martha, Martha," the Lord answered, "you are anxious and upset about many things, but few things are needed—actually, only one. Mary has chosen what is better, and it will not be taken away from her." Luke 10:1, 17-20, 25-42

Someone in the crowd said to Jesus, "Teacher, tell my brother to divide the family property with me."

Jesus answered, "Friend, who made me a judge or arbitrator between the two of you?" Then he said to them, "Watch out! Be careful not to get greedy, because life isn't about how much a person has."

Then Jesus told them a story. He said, "There was a rich man whose land produced a very large crop. He thought to himself, 'What should I do? I don't have anywhere to store all my grain.'

"But then he said, 'I know what I'll do! I'll tear down my barns and build bigger ones, and I'll store my extra grain there. Then I'll tell myself, "You've got enough stored away to last many years. Take it easy. Eat, drink, and have a good time!" '

"But God said to him, 'You foolish man! Tonight, you are going to die. And then who will get all the things you collected for yourself?'

"That's what it will be like for people who store up things for themselves but who aren't rich as far as God is concerned." Luke 12:13-21

Then some people in the crowd told Jesus about what had happened to certain Galileans whose blood Pilate mixed with their sacrifices. Jesus said, "These people from Galilee suffered greatly. But do you think this was because they were worse sinners than all the other Galileans? No, I'm telling you. Unless you turn away from your sins, you will all die too. Or what about those 18 people in Siloam who died when the tower fell on them? Do you think they were more guilty than all the others living in Jerusalem? I tell you, they were not! But unless you turn away from your sins, you will all die too."

Jesus was teaching in one of the synagogues on a Sabbath day. A woman was there who'd been disabled by an evil spirit for 18 years. She was bent over and couldn't stand up straight. Jesus saw her and asked her to come to him. He told her, "Woman, you will no longer be disabled. I'm going to set you free!" Then he put his hands on her, and right away she stood up straight and praised God.

But the synagogue leader was angry because Jesus had healed the woman on the Sabbath day. He told the people, "There are six days for work, so come and be healed on those days. Don't come on the Sabbath day."

The Lord responded, "You're such hypocrites! Doesn't each of you go to the barn and untie your ox or donkey on the Sabbath day, and don't you then lead it out and give it water? So shouldn't this woman, who is a member of Abraham's family line, but who was kept disabled by Satan for 18 long years, have been set free on the Sabbath day from what was keeping her disabled?"

When Jesus said this, all those who opposed him were put to shame. But the people were delighted. They loved all the wonderful things he was doing. Luke 13:1-5, 10-17

As Jesus went along, he saw a man who'd been blind since he was born. His disciples asked him, "Rabbi, was this man born blind because he sinned, or was it because his parents sinned?"

Jesus answered, "This man didn't sin, and his parents didn't sin, either. He was born blind so that God's power could be demonstrated through him. We must do the works of the one who sent me while it's still day. Night is coming, when no one can work. While I am in the world, I am the light of the world."

After he said that, he spit on the ground, made some mud with the spit, and put the mud on the man's eyes. Then he told him, "Go and wash in the Pool of Siloam." (Siloam means Sent.) So the man went and washed, and he came back able to see.

His neighbors and the people who used to watch him begging asked, "Isn't this the same man who used to sit and beg?" Some claimed that it was.

Others said, "No, it only looks like him."

But the man who'd been blind kept saying, "Yes, I'm that man."

"Then how come you can see now?" they asked.

He replied, "The man they call Jesus made some mud and put it on my eyes. He told me to go to Siloam and wash. So I went and washed, and then I could see."

"Where is that man?" they asked.

"I don't know," he said.

They brought the man who'd been blind to the Pharisees. (Jesus had made the mud and restored the man's sight on a Sabbath day.) The Pharisees also asked him how he'd become able to see.

"He put mud on my eyes," the man replied, "and then I washed, and now I can see."

Some of the Pharisees said, "This Jesus is not from God, because he doesn't keep the Sabbath day."

But others asked, "How could a sinner do such signs?" So the Pharisees were divided.

Then they turned again to the blind man. "What do you have to say about him?" they asked. "It was your eyes he opened."

The man answered, "He's a prophet."

They still didn't believe that the man had been blind but could now see. So they sent for his parents. "Is this your son?" they asked. "Is this the one you say was born blind? How is it that now he can see?"

"We know he's our son," the parents answered, "and we know he was born blind. But we don't know how he can see now, and we don't know who restored his sight. Ask him. He's an adult, and he can speak for himself."

His parents said that because they were afraid of the Jewish leaders, who had already decided that anyone who said Jesus was the Messiah would be put out of the synagogue. That was why the man's parents said, "He's an adult; ask him."

The Pharisees called back in the man who'd been blind. "Give glory to God by telling the truth!" they said. "We know that man is a sinner."

"I don't know if he's a sinner or not," he replied, "but I do know one thing. I used to be blind, and now I can see!"

Then they asked him, "What did he do to you? How did he open your eyes?"

He answered, "I've already told you, but you didn't listen. Why do you want to hear it again? Do you want to become his disciples too?"

Then they started to insult him. "You're this man's disciple," they said, "but we're disciples of Moses! We know that God spoke to Moses, but we don't even know where this man comes from."

The man answered, "That's quite a surprise! You don't know where he comes from, and yet he restored my sight. We know that God doesn't listen to sinners. He listens to the godly person who does his will. Nobody has ever heard of anyone making a person who was born blind able to see. If this man hadn't come from God, he wouldn't be able to do anything."

Then the Pharisees replied, "Your parents were living in sin when you were born! You know what that makes you. So how dare you talk to us like that?" And they threw him out of the synagogue.

Jesus heard that the Pharisees had thrown the man out. So he went and found him and asked him, "Do you believe in the Son of Man?"

"Who is he, sir?" the man asked. "Tell me, so I can believe in him."

Jesus said, "You have now seen him. He's the one speaking with you."

Then the man said, "Lord, I believe." And he worshiped him.

Jesus said, "I've come into this world to judge it, so that people who are blind will become able to see and that people who can see will become blind."

Some Pharisees who were with him heard him say this and they asked, "What? Are we blind too?"

Jesus said, "If you were blind, you wouldn't be guilty of sin. But since you claim you can see, you remain guilty. John 9:1-41

"Truly I tell you, anyone who doesn't enter the sheep pen through the gate, but who climbs in by some other way, is a thief and a robber. The one who enters through the gate is the shepherd of the sheep. The gatekeeper opens the gate for him, and the sheep listen to his voice. He calls his own sheep by name, and he leads them out. When he has brought out all his own sheep, he walks on ahead of them, and his sheep follow him, because they know his voice. But they will never follow a stranger. In fact, they will run away, because they don't recognize a stranger's voice."

Jesus was using an example, but the Pharisees didn't understand what he was telling them. So Jesus said again, "Truly I tell you, I am the gate for the sheep. All those who've come before me have been thieves and robbers, but the sheep haven't listened to them. I am the gate; anyone who enters through me will be saved. They will come in and go out and find good places to graze. A thief comes only to steal and kill and destroy. I have come so they may have life and have it in the fullest possible way.

"I am the good shepherd. The good shepherd gives up his life for the sheep. The hired hand isn't the shepherd and doesn't own the sheep. So when he sees a wolf coming, he leaves the sheep and runs away. Then the wolf attacks the flock and scatters it. The man runs away because he's a hired hand and doesn't care about the sheep.

"I am the good shepherd. I know my sheep, and my sheep know me. They know me just as the Father knows me and I know the Father. And I give up my life for the sheep. I have other sheep who aren't in this sheep pen. I must bring them in too. They will also listen to my voice, and then there will be one flock and one shepherd.

"The reason my Father loves me is that I give up my life. But I will get it back again. No one takes it from me; I give it up myself. I have the authority to give it up, and I have the authority to take it back. This is the command I received from my Father."

The Jews who heard these words disagreed with each other. Many of them said, "He's controlled by a demon! He's gone crazy! Why should we listen to him?"

But others said, "A person controlled by a demon doesn't say things like this. Can a demon restore the sight of someone who's blind?"

In the winter, during the Feast of Hanukkah at Jerusalem, Jesus was in the temple courtyard, walking through Solomon's Porch. The

Jewish leaders surrounded him and demanded, "How long are you going to keep us in suspense? If you're the Messiah, come right out and say so."

Jesus answered, "I did say so, but you didn't believe me. The works that I do in my Father's name are a witness for me. But you don't believe, because you're not my sheep. My sheep listen to my voice. I know them, and they follow me. I give them eternal life, and they will never die. No one will steal them out of my hand. My Father, who has given them to me, is greater than anyone. No one can steal them out of my Father's hand. I and the Father are one."

Once again the Jewish leaders picked up stones to kill him. But Jesus said to them, "I've shown you many good works from the Father. Which good work are you going to throw stones at me for?"

"We're not going to throw stones at you for any good work," they answered. "We're going to stone you because you claim to be God when you're only a man."

Jesus answered them, "Isn't it written in your Law, 'I have said you are "gods" '? We know that Scripture is always true. If God could speak to some people and call them 'gods,' then what about the one the Father set apart as his very own and sent into the world? Why do you accuse me of doing wrong because I said, 'I am God's Son'? Don't believe me unless I do the works of my Father. But if I do them, even if you don't believe me, believe the works. Then you will know and understand that the Father is in me and I am in the Father."

They tried again to arrest him, but he escaped from them.

Then Jesus went back across the Jordan River to the place where John had been baptizing in the early days. He stayed there and many people came to him. They said, "John never performed a sign, but everything he said about this man was true." And in that place many people believed in Jesus. John 10:1-42

CHAPTER 13

RAISING THE DEAD

Then Jesus went through the towns and villages, teaching the people as he continued on his way to Jerusalem. Someone asked him, "Lord, are only a few people going to be saved?"

He said to them, "Try very hard to enter through the narrow door. I tell you that many will try to enter, but they will not be able to. Once the owner of the house gets up and closes the door, you will have to stand outside knocking and begging, 'Sir, open the door for us.'

"But he will answer, 'I don't know you and I don't know where you're from.'

"Then you will say, 'We ate and drank with you. You taught in our streets.'

"But he will repeat, 'I don't know you and I don't know where you're from. Get away from me, all you who do evil!'

"You will weep and grind your teeth together when you see Abraham, Isaac, and Jacob and all the prophets in God's kingdom while you yourselves are thrown out. People will come from east and west and north and south to take their places at the feast in God's kingdom. Then the last will be first and the first will be last."

At that time some Pharisees came to Jesus and said to him, "Leave this place and go somewhere else, because Herod wants to kill you."

He replied, "Go and tell that fox, 'Today and tomorrow I will keep on driving out demons and healing people, and on the third day I will reach my goal.' In any case, I must keep going today and tomorrow and the next day. Certainly no prophet can die outside Jerusalem!

"Jerusalem! Jerusalem! You kill the prophets and throw stones to kill those who are sent to you. Many times I've wanted to gather your people together, as a hen gathers her chicks under her wings, but you would not let me. Look, your house is left empty. I tell you, you will not see me again until you say, 'Blessed is the one who comes in the name of the Lord.' " Luke 13:22-35

One Sabbath day, Jesus went to eat in the house of a well-known Pharisee. While he was there, he was being carefully watched. In front of him there was a man whose body was badly swollen. Jesus turned to the Pharisees and the experts in the law and asked them, "Is it breaking the Law to heal on the Sabbath day?"

But they didn't say anything. So Jesus took hold of the man, healed him, and sent him on his way.

He asked them another question. He said, "If you had a child or an ox that fell into a well on the Sabbath day, wouldn't you pull them out right away?"

And they had nothing to say.

Jesus noticed how the guests picked the places of honor at the table, so he told them a story. He said, "Suppose someone invites you to a wedding feast. Don't take the place of honor, because a person more important than you may have been invited. If so, the host who invited both of you will come to you and say, 'Give this person your seat.' Then you'll be humiliated, and you'll have to take the least important place. So when you're invited somewhere, take the lowest place. Your host will come over to you and say, 'Friend, move up to a better place.' Then you'll be honored in front of all the other guests. All who lift themselves up will be humbled, but those who humble themselves will be lifted up."

Then Jesus spoke to his host. "When you give a lunch or a dinner, don't invite your friends, your brothers or sisters, your relatives, or your rich neighbors. If you do, they may invite you to eat with them in return and you will be paid back. When you give a banquet, invite the poor and those who can't see or walk. Then you will be blessed. Your guests won't be able to pay you back, but you will be paid back when those who are right with God are raised from the dead."

One of the people at the table with him heard these things and he said to Jesus, "Blessed is the one who will eat at the feast in God's kingdom."

Jesus responded, "A certain man was preparing a great banquet and he invited many guests. When the day of the banquet arrived, he sent a servant to get those he had invited. The servant told them, 'Come, because everything is now ready.'

"But they all began to make excuses. The first one said, 'I've just bought a field and I have to go see it. Please excuse me.'

"Another one said, 'I've just bought five pairs of oxen and I'm on my way to try them out. Please excuse me.'

"Still another said, 'I just got married, so I can't come.'

"The servant came back and reported this to his master. Then the owner of the house became angry and ordered his servant, 'Quick! Go into the streets and alleys of the town and bring in the poor and those who can't see or walk.'

"The servant came back and said, 'Sir, what you ordered has been done, but there's still room.'

"Then the master told his servant, 'Go out to the roads and country lanes and make people come in. I want my house to be full. But I tell you, not one of those people I first invited will get a taste of my banquet.' "

Large crowds were traveling with Jesus. He turned to them and said, "Anyone who comes to me but doesn't love me more than their father and mother, their wife and children, their brothers and sisters, and even their own life can't be my disciple. Whoever doesn't carry their cross and follow me can't be my disciple.

"Suppose one of you wants to build a tower. Won't you sit down first and figure out how much it will cost? Then you'll know whether you have enough money to finish it. If you start building but aren't able to finish, everyone who sees it will laugh at you. They'll say, 'This person started to build but wasn't able to finish.'

"Or suppose a king is about to go to war against another king. Won't he first sit down and think about whether he can win if he only has 10,000 soldiers while the other king has 20,000? If he decides he can't win, he'll send messengers to make a peace treaty with the other king while he's still far away. You have to ask the same kind of question, because if you don't give up everything you have, you can't be my disciple." Luke 14:1-33

Because the tax collectors and sinners were all gathering around to hear Jesus, the Pharisees and the teachers of the law started muttering, "This man welcomes sinners and eats with them."

So Jesus told them a story. He said, "Suppose one of you has 100 sheep and loses one of them. Won't he leave the 99 in the open country and go and look for the one lost sheep until he finds it? And when he finds it, he'll put it on his shoulders happily and go home. Then he'll call his friends and neighbors together and say, 'Celebrate with me, I've found the sheep that was lost!' I tell you, it will be the same in heaven. There will be more celebration for one sinner who turns away from sin than for 99 godly people who don't have sins they need to turn away from.

"Or suppose a woman has ten silver coins and loses one. Won't she light a lamp, sweep the house, and search carefully until she finds it? And when she does find it, she'll call her friends and neighbors together and say, 'Celebrate with me, I've found my lost coin!' I tell you, it's the same in heaven. There's celebration in heaven over one sinner who turns away from sin."

Jesus continued, "There was a man who had two sons. The younger son said to his father, 'Father, give me my share of the family property.' So the father divided the property between his two sons.

"Not long after that, the younger son packed up everything he had, went to a distant country, and wasted his money on extravagant living. But after he'd spent everything, there was a famine in that area, and he began to go hungry. The son went to work for a citizen of the country, who sent him out to the fields to feed his pigs. Still, no one gave him anything to eat, and he wished he could fill his stomach with the husks the pigs were eating.

"Then he came to his senses and said, 'All of my father's hired servants have more than enough to eat, so why am I starving to death here? I'll get up and go back to my father and tell him, "Father, I've sinned against heaven and against you, and I don't deserve to be considered your son anymore. Please let me be like one of your hired servants." ' So he got up and went to his father.

"But while he was still a long way off, his father saw him and was filled with tender love for him. He ran to his son, threw his arms around him, and kissed him.

"The son began, 'Father, I've sinned against heaven and against you, and I don't deserve to be considered your son anymore.'

"But the father said to his servants, 'Quick! Bring the best robe and put it on him. Put a ring on his finger and sandals on his feet. Bring the fattened calf and kill it. Let's have a feast and celebrate, because this son of mine was dead, but now he's alive. He was lost, but now he has been found.' So they began to celebrate.

"Meanwhile the older son was in the field. When he came near the house, he heard music and dancing. So he called one of the servants and asked him what was going on. 'Your brother has come home,' the servant replied. 'Your father has killed the fattened calf because he's back safe and sound.'

"The older brother became angry and refused to go in. So his father went out and pleaded with him. But he answered his father, 'Look! All these years I've worked like a slave for you. I've always obeyed your orders. But you've never given me even a young goat so I could celebrate with my friends. But when this son of yours comes home after wasting your money on prostitutes, you kill the fattened calf for him!'

"'My son,' the father said, 'you are always with me, and everything I have is yours. But we had to celebrate and be glad, because this brother of yours was dead, but now he's alive again; he was lost, but now he has been found.'" Luke 15:1-32

Jesus told his disciples another story. He said, "There was a rich man whose manager was accused of wasting what the rich man owned. The rich man called him in and said, 'What's this I hear about you? Turn in your accounts, because you can't be my manager anymore.'

"The manager said to himself, 'What am I going to do now? My master is taking away my job. I'm not strong enough to dig, and I'm too ashamed to beg. I know—I'll do something so that when I lose my job here, people will welcome me into their houses.'

"So he called in each person who owed his master something. He asked the first one, 'How much do you owe my master?'

"'I owe 900 gallons of olive oil,' he replied.

"The manager told him, 'Take your bill, sit down quickly, and change it to 450 gallons.'

"Then he asked the second one, 'And how much do you owe?'

"'I owe 1,000 bushels of wheat,' he replied.

"The manager told him, 'Take your bill and change it to 800 bushels.'

"Even though the manager had not been honest, the master praised him for being clever. The people of this world are more clever in dealing with their own kind than God's people are. I tell you, use the riches of this world to make friends for yourselves.

Then when your riches are gone, you will be welcomed into an eternal home.

"If you can be trusted with very little, then you can also be trusted with a lot. But if you aren't honest with very little, then you also won't be honest with a lot. If you aren't trustworthy in handling worldly wealth, who will trust you with genuine riches? If you aren't trustworthy in handling someone else's property, who will give you property of your own?

"No one can serve two masters at the same time. Either you will hate the first and love the second, or you will be faithful to the first and dislike the second. You can't serve God and money at the same time."

But when the Pharisees, who loved money, heard all that Jesus said, they sneered at him.

Jesus told them, "You try to make yourselves look good in the eyes of other people, but God knows your hearts. There are things that people value highly that God can't stand.

"Once there was a rich man who dressed in purple clothes and fine linen. He lived an easy life every day. A beggar named Lazarus used to sit at his gate. His body was covered with sores, and the dogs would come and lick them. Lazarus would have been happy just to eat what fell from the rich man's table.

"When the time came for the beggar to die, the angels carried him to Abraham's side. The rich man also died and was buried. In the land of the dead, the rich man was suffering terribly. He looked up and saw Abraham far away, with Lazarus by his side. So the rich man called out, 'Father Abraham, have pity on me! Send Lazarus to dip the tip of his finger in water and cool my tongue, because I'm in terrible pain in this fire.'

"But Abraham replied, 'Son, remember that in your lifetime you received good things, while Lazarus received bad things. Now he is comforted here while you are in terrible pain. Besides, a wide space has been placed between us and you, so that even if we want to, we can't go from here to you, and no one can cross over from you to us.'

"The rich man answered, 'Then I beg you, father Abraham, send Lazarus to my family. I have five brothers. Let Lazarus warn them so that they won't come to this place of terrible suffering.'

"Abraham replied, 'They have the teachings of Moses and the Prophets. Let your brothers listen to them.'

" 'They won't, father Abraham,' he said. 'But if someone from the dead goes to them, then they will turn away from their sins.'

"Abraham said to him, 'If they won't listen to Moses and the Prophets, they won't be convinced even if someone rises from the dead.' " Luke 16:1-15, 19-31

The apostles said to the Lord, "Help us to have more faith!"

He replied, "If you have faith even as small as a mustard seed, you can say to this mulberry tree, 'Be pulled up and planted in the sea,' and it will obey you.

"Suppose one of you has a servant who's out plowing or looking after the sheep. When that servant comes in from the field, will you say to him, 'Come along now and sit down to eat'? No, instead you'll say, 'Prepare my supper, dress as a table servant, and wait on me while I eat and drink. Then after that you can eat and drink.' Will you thank the servant because he did what he was told to do? In the same way, when you've done everything you were told to do, you should say, 'We don't deserve a reward, we've only done our duty.' " Luke 17:5-10

A man named Lazarus was sick. He was in Bethany, the village where Mary and her sister Martha lived. Mary would later pour perfume on the Lord and wipe his feet with her hair. Lazarus, who was sick in bed, was her brother. So the sisters sent a message to Jesus. "Lord," they told him, "the one you love is sick."

When Jesus heard this, he said, "This sickness will not end in death. No, it is for God's glory, so that God's Son can receive glory because of it." Jesus loved Martha and her sister and Lazarus, but even after he learned that Lazarus was sick, he stayed where he was for two more days. Then he said to his disciples, "Let's go back to Judea."

"Rabbi," they objected, "the Jews there were just trying to kill you with stones. And now you want to go back?"

Jesus answered, "Aren't there 12 hours of daylight? Anyone who walks during the day doesn't trip and fall, because they can see by this world's light. It's the person who walks at night who trips and falls, because they don't have any light."

After he'd said that, Jesus told them, "Our friend Lazarus has fallen asleep, but I'm going there to wake him up."

His disciples responded, "Lord, if he's sleeping, that means he'll get better." Jesus had meant that Lazarus was dead, but his disciples thought he'd meant that Lazarus had actually fallen asleep.

So then he came right out and told them, "Lazarus is dead. For your sake, I'm glad I wasn't there, because now you'll believe. Let's go to him."

Then Thomas, who was also called Didymus, said to the rest of the disciples, "Let's go along, so we can die with him."

When Jesus arrived, he found out that Lazarus had already been in the tomb for four days. Bethany was less than two miles from Jerusalem, and many Jews had come out to comfort Martha and Mary on the loss of their brother. When Martha heard that Jesus was coming, she went out to meet him, but Mary stayed at home.

Martha said to Jesus, "Lord, if you had been here, my brother would not have died. But I know that even now God will give you anything you ask for."

Jesus said to her, "Your brother will rise again."

Martha answered, "I know he will rise again when people are raised from the dead on the last day."

Jesus said to her, "I am the resurrection and the life. Anyone who believes in me will live, even if they die. And whoever lives by believing in me will never die. Do you believe this?"

"Yes, Lord," she replied, "I believe that you are the Messiah, the Son of God who has come into the world."

After she said this, she went back home and called her sister Mary aside to speak with her. "The Teacher is here," she said, "and he's asking for you."

When Mary heard this, she got up quickly and went out to meet him. Jesus hadn't yet entered the village; he was still at the place where Martha had met him. When the Jews who'd been comforting Mary in the house noticed that she'd gotten up quickly and gone out, they followed her. They thought she was going to the tomb to mourn there.

When Mary reached the place where Jesus was and she saw him, she knelt down in front of him. "Lord," she said, "if you had been here, my brother would not have died."

When Jesus saw her crying, and he also saw the Jews who'd come along with her crying, it made him angry and distressed that death caused so much sorrow. "Where have you put him?" he asked.

They answered, "Lord, come and see."

Jesus wept.

Then the Jews said, "See how much he loved him!"

But some of them said, "He opened the eyes of the blind man. Couldn't he have kept this man from dying?"

Jesus came to the tomb, which was a cave with a stone in front of the entrance, and once again he was distressed. "Take away the stone," he said.

"But, Lord," said Martha, the sister of the dead man, "by this time there will be a bad smell, because Lazarus has been in that tomb for four days."

Jesus responded, "Didn't I tell you that if you believed, you would see God's glory?"

So they took away the stone. Then Jesus looked up and said, "Father, I thank you for hearing me. I know that you always hear me, but I'm saying this for the benefit of the people standing here, so they'll believe that you've sent me."

Then Jesus called out in a loud voice, "Lazarus, come out!" And the dead man came out. His hands and feet were wrapped with strips of linen and there was a cloth around his face.

Jesus said to them, "Unwrap him and let him go."

Many of the Jews who'd come to visit Mary saw what Jesus did, and they believed in him. But some of them went to the Pharisees and told them what Jesus had done. Then the chief priests and the Pharisees called a meeting of the Sanhedrin, the council of elders.

They asked, "What are we supposed to do with this man? He's performing many signs. If we let him keep doing that, everyone will believe in him. Then the Romans will come and destroy our temple and our nation."

Then one of them named Caiaphas spoke up. He was the high priest that year. He said, "You don't know anything at all! You don't realize that it's better for you if one man dies for the people than if the whole nation is destroyed."

He didn't say this on his own. Rather, as the high priest that year, he was prophesying that Jesus would die for the Jewish nation— and not only for that nation, but for God's children scattered everywhere. Jesus' death would bring them together and make them one.

So from that day on, the Jewish rulers planned to kill Jesus. As a result, Jesus no longer moved around openly among the people of Judea. Instead, he went away to an area near the desert, to a village called Ephraim. He stayed there with his disciples. John 11:1-54

CHAPTER 14

WELCOMED AS KING

When it was almost time for the Jewish Passover Feast, many people went up from the countryside to Jerusalem for the special washing that would make them pure before the feast. They kept looking for Jesus. As they stood in the temple courtyard, they asked one another, "What do you think? Isn't he coming to the feast at all?" The chief priests and Pharisees had ordered that anyone who found out where Jesus was staying had to report it so they could arrest him. John 11:55-57

On his way to Jerusalem, Jesus traveled along the border between Samaria and Galilee. As he was going into a village, ten men who had a skin disease met him. They kept their distance but called out in a loud voice, "Jesus! Master! Have pity on us!"

Jesus saw them and said, "Go show yourselves to the priests." And while they were on their way, they were healed.

When one of them saw that he had been healed, he came back, praising God in a loud voice. He threw himself at Jesus' feet and thanked him. This man was a Samaritan.

Jesus asked, "Weren't all ten healed? Where are the other nine? Isn't anyone else going to return and praise God except this foreigner?" Then Jesus said to him, "Stand up and go, your faith has healed you."

Once the Pharisees asked Jesus when God's kingdom would come. He answered, "The coming of God's kingdom isn't something you can see, and people won't say, 'Here it is,' or, 'There it is.' That's because God's kingdom is among you."

Then Jesus said to his disciples, "The time is coming when you will long to see one of the days of the Son of Man, but you won't see it. People will tell you, 'There he is!' or, 'Here he is!' But don't go running off after them, because when the Son of Man comes, he will be like lightning that flashes and lights up the sky from one end to the other. But first the Son of Man must suffer many things and be rejected by the people of this generation.

"Remember how it was in the days of Noah; it will be the same when the Son of Man comes. People were eating and drinking, getting married and giving their daughters in marriage, right up to the day when Noah entered the ark. Then the flood came and destroyed them all.

"It was the same in the days of Lot. People were eating and drinking, buying and selling, planting and building. But on the day Lot left Sodom, fire and sulfur rained down from heaven, and all the people were destroyed.

"It will be just like that on the day the Son of Man is shown to the world. On that day, if anyone is on the housetop, they shouldn't go down to get their things from inside the house. No one who's in the field should go back for anything either. Remember Lot's wife! Whoever tries to keep their life will lose it, but whoever loses their life will keep it. I tell you, on that night two people will be in one bed; one will be taken and the other will be left. Two women will be grinding grain together; one will be taken and the other will be left." Luke 17:11-36

Then Jesus told his disciples a story to show them that they should always pray and not give up. He said, "In a certain town there was a judge who didn't have any respect for God and who didn't care what people thought. A widow lived in that town and she came to the judge again and again, begging him, 'Defend me against the person who's doing me wrong!'

"For some time the judge refused, but he finally said to himself, 'Though I don't have any respect for God and I don't care what people think, because this widow keeps bothering me, I'm going to see that things are made right for her. If I don't, someday she'll pester me to death!' "

The Lord said, "Listen to what the unfair judge says. And won't God make things right for his chosen people, who cry out to him day and night? Will he keep putting them off? I tell you, God will see that things are made right for them, and he'll make sure that it happens quickly. But when the Son of Man comes, will he find people on earth who have faith?"

Jesus told a story to some people who were sure they were right with God and looked down on everyone else. He said to them, "Two men went up to the temple to pray. One was a Pharisee and the other was a tax collector. The Pharisee stood by himself and prayed, 'God, I thank you that I'm not like other people—not like robbers, or people who do other evil things, or those who commit adultery, or even like this tax collector. I fast twice a week and I give a tenth of everything I get.'

"But the tax collector stood off by himself and wouldn't even look up to heaven. He struck his chest in remorse and prayed, 'God, have mercy on me. I'm a sinner.'

"I tell you, the tax collector went home accepted by God, but the Pharisee didn't. All those who lift themselves up will be humbled, but those who humble themselves will be lifted up." Luke 18:1-14

When Jesus had finished saying these things, he left Galilee and went into the area of Judea that's on the other side of the Jordan River. Large crowds followed him, and he healed many people there.

Some Pharisees came to test Jesus. They asked, "Does the Law allow a man to divorce his wife for any reason he wants?"

Jesus replied, "Haven't you read that in the beginning the Creator 'made them male and female'? He said, 'A man will leave his father and mother and be joined to his wife, and the two will become one.' Since they are no longer two, but one, no one should separate what God has joined together."

They asked, "Then why did Moses say that a man could give his wife a letter of divorce and send her away?"

Jesus replied, "Moses allowed you to divorce your wives because you were so hard-hearted. But that's not the way it was from the beginning. I tell you that anyone who divorces his wife, unless she has been unfaithful, and marries another woman commits adultery."

The disciples said to him. "If that's the way it is between a husband and a wife, then it's better not to get married."

Jesus answered, "Not everyone can grasp this saying. God has to enable a person to do that. Others won't get married, either because they were born unable to have children or because other people made them that way. Still others will choose not to get married so they can serve the kingdom of heaven single. But anyone who can grasp the saying should accept it." Matt. 19:1-12

As Jesus started on his way, a man ran up to him and got down on his knees in front of him. "Good teacher," he asked, "what must I do to receive eternal life?"

"Why do you call me good?" Jesus replied. "No one is good except God. You know what the commandments say. 'Do not murder, do not commit adultery, do not steal, don't be a false witness, don't cheat, honor your father and mother.'"

"Teacher," he said eagerly, "I've obeyed all those commandments since I was a boy."

Jesus looked at him and loved him. "You're missing one thing," he said. "Go, sell everything you have and give the money to the poor, and you'll have treasure in heaven. Then come and follow me."

When the man heard that, he looked gloomy, and he went away sad, because he was very rich.

Jesus looked around and said to his disciples, "How hard it is for rich people to enter the kingdom of God!"

The disciples were amazed at what he said. But Jesus said again, "Children, how hard it is to enter the kingdom of God! It's easier for a camel to go through the eye of a needle than for someone who's rich to enter the kingdom of God!"

The disciples were even more amazed, and they said to each other, "Then who can be saved?"

Jesus looked at them and said, "With people, it's impossible, but not with God. All things are possible with God."

Then Peter spoke up. "We've left everything to follow you!" he said.

"Truly I tell you," Jesus responded, "anyone who has left home or family or fields for me and the good news will receive 100 times as much in this world. They will have other homes, brothers, sisters, mothers, children, and fields—and they'll also be systematically oppressed by others. But in the world to come they'll live forever. Mark 10:17-30

"The kingdom of heaven is like the manager of an estate who went out early in the morning to hire workers for his vineyard. He agreed to give them the usual pay for a day's work, and he sent them into the vineyard.

"About nine o'clock, he went out again and saw others standing in the market doing nothing. He told them, 'You also go and work in my vineyard, and I'll pay you what's fair.' So they went.

"He went out again at about noon and at three o'clock and did the same thing. About five o'clock he went out and found others still standing around. He asked them, 'Why have you been standing here all day doing nothing?'

" 'Because no one has hired us,' they answered.

"He said to them, 'You go and work in my vineyard too.'

"When evening came, the manager of the vineyard told his foreman, 'Call the workers in and give them their pay. Begin with the ones I hired last and end with the ones I hired first.'

"When the workers who'd been hired at about five o'clock came in, each one was given the usual pay for a whole day. So when those who'd been hired first came in, they expected to receive more. But each of them also received a day's pay. When they saw what they were getting, they began to complain about the manager. 'Those people who were hired last only worked for one hour,' they said. 'But you paid them the same as us, even though we did most of the work and were out in the hot sun all day.'

"The manager answered one of them, 'I'm not being unfair to you, my friend. Didn't you agree to work for the usual day's pay? Take your money and go. I want to give the ones I hired last the same pay I gave you. Don't I have the right to do what I want with my own money? Why should you feel cheated just because I was generous to the others?'

"So those who are last will be first, and those who are first will be last." Matt. 20:1-16

They were on their way up to Jerusalem, with Jesus leading the way. The disciples were amazed, and the crowd that was following along was afraid.

Jesus took his 12 disciples to one side and told them again what was going to happen to him. "We're going up to Jerusalem," he said, "where the Son of Man is going to be handed over to the chief priests and the teachers of the law. They will sentence him to death and hand him over to the Gentiles, who will humiliate him and spit on him, whip him and kill him. But three days later, he will rise from the dead!"

James and John, the sons of Zebedee, came to Jesus and said, "Teacher, we'd like to ask you for a favor."

"What do you want me to do for you?" he replied.

They answered, "In your glorious kingdom, let one of us sit at your right hand and the other at your left hand."

"You don't know what you're asking for," Jesus responded. "Can you drink the cup I'm going to drink? Can you go through the baptism I have to go through?"

"We can," they answered.

Jesus told them, "You will drink the cup that I drink, and you will go through the baptism that I go through. But it's not for me to say who will sit at my right or left hand. These places belong to the ones they've been prepared for."

When the other ten disciples heard about this, they got angry with James and John. But Jesus called them all together and said, "You know that the leaders of the Gentiles like to use their power over others and that their high officials order people around. Don't be like that. Instead, any of you who wants to be great among you must become your servant, and anyone who wants to be first must be a slave to all the others. Even the Son of Man didn't come to be served, but to serve others and to give his life to set many people free." Mark 10:32-45

As Jesus was approaching Jericho, a man who was blind was sitting by the side of the road begging. The man heard the crowd going by and asked what was happening. They told him, "Jesus of Nazareth is passing by."

So he called out, "Jesus! Son of David! Have mercy on me!"

Those leading the crowd spoke harshly to him and told him to be quiet. But he shouted even louder, "Son of David! Have mercy on me!"

Jesus stopped and told the people to bring the man over to him. When he came near, Jesus asked him, "What do you want me to do for you?"

The man who was blind replied, "Lord, I want to be able to see."

Jesus said to him, "Receive your sight. Your faith has healed you!"

Right away he became able to see and he followed Jesus, praising God. When all the people saw this, they also praised God. Luke 18:35-43

Jesus then entered Jericho and started to pass through the city. A man named Zacchaeus lived there. He was a chief tax collector and he was very rich. Zacchaeus wanted to see who Jesus was, but he was a short man, and he couldn't see Jesus because of the crowd. So he ran ahead and climbed a sycamore-fig tree so he could see Jesus, since Jesus was coming that way.

When Jesus reached the spot where Zacchaeus was, he looked up and said, "Zacchaeus, come down at once! I must stay at your house today."

He did come down at once, and he welcomed Jesus gladly. When all the people saw this, they began to whisper among themselves, "Jesus has gone to be the guest of a sinner."

But at dinner, Zacchaeus stood up and said, "Look, Lord! Here and now I give half of what I own to the poor. And if I have cheated anybody out of anything, I will pay back four times the amount I took."

Jesus said to him, "Today salvation has come to this house, because you, too, are a member of Abraham's family line. The Son of Man has come to look for the lost and to save them."

While the people were listening to these things, Jesus told them a story, because he was near Jerusalem, and the people thought that God's kingdom was going to appear right away.

Jesus said, "A man from an important family went to a country far away to be made king and to return home to his subjects after that. He sent for ten of his slaves and gave each of them about three months' worth of wages. 'Put this money to work until I come back,' he said.

"But the people who were going to be his subjects hated him. They sent some messengers after him to say, 'We don't want this man to be our king.'

"But he was made king anyway, and he then returned home. He sent for the slaves he'd given the money to, because he wanted to find out what they'd earned with it.

"The first one came to him and said, 'Sir, your money has earned ten times as much.'

" 'You have done well, my good slave!' his master replied. 'Because you have shown that you are faithful through this very small matter, I'm going to put you in charge of ten towns.'

"The second slave came to his master and said, 'Sir, your money has earned five times as much.'

"His master answered, 'I'm going to put you in charge of five towns.'

"Then another slave came and said, 'Sir, here is your money. I kept it hidden in a piece of cloth. I was afraid of you, because you are a hard man. You take out what you did not put in and you harvest what you did not plant.'

"His master replied, 'I will judge you by your own words, you worthless slave! So you knew that I'm a hard man? You knew that I take out what I didn't put in and that I harvest what I didn't plant? Then why didn't you put my money in the bank? That way I could have collected it with interest when I came back.'

"Then he said to those standing by, 'Take his money away from him and give it to the one who has ten times as much.'

" 'Sir,' they said, 'he already has ten times as much!'

"The master replied, 'I tell you that to everyone who has, more will be given. But as for those who have nothing, even what they do have will be taken away from them. And now for those enemies of mine who didn't want me to be their king—bring them here and kill them in front of me!' " Luke 19:1-27

As they approached Jerusalem, they came to Bethphage on the Mount of Olives. Jesus sent out two disciples, telling them, "Go to the village ahead of you. As soon as you get there, you'll find a donkey tied up, with her colt next to her. Untie them and bring them to me.

If anyone says anything to you, tell them, 'The Lord needs them.' The owner will send them right away."

This happened to make the words of the prophet come true: "Say to the city of Zion, 'See, your king is coming to you, gentle and riding on a donkey, riding on a donkey's colt.'"

The disciples went and did what Jesus had told them to do. They brought the donkey and the colt and placed their coats on them for Jesus to sit on. A very large crowd spread their coats on the road, while others cut branches from the trees and spread those on the road. Some of the people went ahead of him, and some followed behind, and they all shouted: "Hosanna to the Son of David! Blessed is the one who comes in the name of the Lord! Hosanna in the highest heaven!" Matt. 21:1-9

Some of the Pharisees in the crowd said to Jesus, "Teacher, tell your disciples to stop shouting!"

"I tell you," he responded, "if they keep quiet, the stones will cry out." Luke 19:39-40

At first, Jesus' disciples didn't understand all this. They only realized after he was glorified that these things had been written about him and that they had been done to him.

The crowd that had been with Jesus when he called Lazarus from the tomb and raised him from the dead continued to tell everyone about what had happened. Many people went out to meet him because they'd heard that he had done this sign. So the Pharisees said to one another, "Look, we aren't getting anywhere. See how the whole world is following him!" John 12:16-19

CHAPTER 15

AUTHORITY QUESTIONED

As Jesus approached Jerusalem and saw the city, he began to weep. He said, "I wish you had known this day what would bring you peace! But now it is hidden from your eyes. The days will come when your enemies will build a wall of dirt up against your city and surround you and close in on you from every side. Because you didn't recognize the time when God came to you, your enemies will smash you to the ground. They will destroy you and all the people inside your walls, and they won't leave one stone on top of another." Luke 19:41-44

Jesus entered Jerusalem and went into the temple courtyard. He looked around at everything, but since it was already late, he went back out to Bethany with the 12 disciples.

The next day, as they were leaving Bethany, they were hungry. Off in the distance Jesus saw a fig tree that was full of leaves. He went over to see if it had any fruit. But when he got there, all he found was leaves, because it wasn't time for figs to ripen yet. Then Jesus said to the tree, "May no one ever eat fruit from you again!" And his disciples heard him say it.

When Jesus got to Jerusalem, he entered the temple courtyard and began to drive out those who were buying and selling there. He turned over the tables of the people who were exchanging money and the benches of those who were selling doves. He wouldn't allow anyone to carry items for sale through the temple courtyard.

Then he taught them, saying, "It is written that the Lord said, 'My house will be called a house where people from all nations can pray.' But you've made it a 'den for robbers.'"

When the chief priests and the teachers of the law heard about this, they began to look for a way to kill Jesus. They were afraid of him, because the whole crowd was amazed at his teaching. Mark 11:11-18

Then the Jewish leaders asked him, "What sign can you show us to prove that you have the right to do this?"

Jesus answered them, "Destroy this temple, and I will raise it up again in three days."

They answered, "It has taken 46 years to build this temple. Are you going to raise it up in three days?"

But the temple Jesus was speaking about was his body. After he had been raised from the dead, his disciples remembered what he had said. Then they believed the Scripture and the words Jesus had spoken. John 2:18-22

There were some Greeks among the people who'd gone up to Jerusalem for the Passover Feast. They came to Philip, who was from Bethsaida in Galilee, to ask for a favor. "Sir," they said, "we'd like to meet Jesus."

Philip went and told this to Andrew, and then the two of them went and told Jesus.

He responded, "The time has come for the Son of Man to receive glory. Truly I tell you, unless a grain of wheat falls to the ground and dies, it remains a single seed. But if it dies, it produces many seeds. Anyone who loves their life will lose it, but anyone who hates their life in this world will keep it and gain eternal life. Anyone who serves me must follow me. Where I am, my servant will also be. My Father will honor the one who serves me.

"But now I'm deeply distressed. What should I say? 'Father, keep me from having to go through with this'? No, this is the very reason why I've come to this point in my life. Father, bring glory to your name!"

Then a voice came from heaven and said, "I have brought glory to my name, and I will bring glory to it again." The crowd there heard the voice. Some said it was thunder, while others said that an angel had spoken to Jesus.

Jesus told them, "That voice was for your benefit, not mine. Now is the time for the world to be judged and for the prince of this world to be thrown out. I'm going to be lifted up from the earth, and when I am, I will draw all people to myself." He said this to indicate what kind of death he was going to die.

The crowd spoke up and asked, "The Law tells us that the Messiah will remain forever, so how can you say, 'The Son of Man must be lifted up'? Who is this 'Son of Man'?"

Then Jesus told them, "You're going to have the light just a little while longer. Walk while you have the light, before darkness catches up with you. Whoever walks in the dark doesn't know where they're going. While you have the light, believe in it, so that you can become children of light."

When Jesus had finished speaking, he left and hid from them.

Even after Jesus had performed so many signs right in front of them, they still wouldn't believe in him. This made the words of Isaiah the prophet come true. He had said, "Lord, who has believed what we've been saying? Who has seen the Lord's saving power?" For this reason, they could not believe. As Isaiah says in another place, "The Lord has blinded their eyes, and he has closed their minds, so they can't see with their eyes, and they can't understand with their minds or turn to the Lord—if they could, he would heal them." Isaiah said this because he saw Jesus' glory and spoke about him.

However, many did believe in him, even among the Jewish leaders. But because of the Pharisees, they wouldn't admit openly that they believed. They were afraid that they'd be thrown out of the synagogue. They loved praise from people more than praise from God.

Then Jesus cried out, "Whoever believes in me doesn't believe only in me, but also in the one who sent me. The one who looks at me sees the one who sent me. I have come into the world to be its light, so that no one who believes in me will remain in darkness.

"If a person hears my words but doesn't obey them, I don't judge that person. I didn't come to judge the world, I came to save the world. But there is a judge for anyone who doesn't accept me and my words. The words I've spoken will judge them on the last day. I haven't spoken on my own. The Father who sent me has commanded me to say everything I've said. I know that his command leads to eternal life, so everything I say is just what the Father has told me to say." John 12:20-50

When evening came, Jesus and his disciples left the city. In the morning, as Jesus and his disciples were walking along, they saw the fig tree again. It was dried up all the way down to its roots. Peter remembered what had happened the day before, and he said to Jesus, "Rabbi, look! The fig tree you put a curse on has dried up!"

"Have faith in God," Jesus said. "Truly I tell you, if anyone says to this mountain, 'Go and throw yourself into the sea,' if they don't doubt in their heart but believe that what they say will happen, it will be done for them. So I tell you, when you pray for something, believe that you have already received it. Then it will be yours. And when you stand praying, forgive anyone you have anything against. That way your Father in heaven will forgive your sins." Mark 11:19-26

Jesus went into the temple courtyard and started teaching there. The chief priests and elders of the people came up to him and asked, "By what authority are you doing these things? Who gave you this authority?"

Jesus answered, "I'll ask you a question too. If you answer me, I'll tell you by what authority I'm doing these things. Where did John's baptism come from? Was it from heaven, or was he acting on human authority?"

They talked this over among themselves and realized, "If we say, 'From heaven,' he'll ask, 'Then why didn't you believe him?' But if we say, 'On human authority,' who knows what the people might do to us? They all believe that John was a prophet."

So they answered Jesus, "We don't know."

Jesus replied, "Then I won't tell you by what authority I'm doing these things either."

"What do you think about this? A certain man had two sons. He went to the first one and said, 'Son, go and work in the vineyard today.'

" 'I won't,' the son answered. But later he changed his mind and went.

"Then the father went to the other son and said the same thing. That son answered, 'I will, sir.' But he didn't go.

"Which of the two sons did what his father wanted?"

"The first," they answered.

Jesus said to them, "Truly I tell you, tax collectors and prostitutes will enter the kingdom of God ahead of you. John came to show you the right way, and you didn't believe him. But the tax collectors and the prostitutes did. Even when you saw that, you didn't turn away from your sins and believe him.

"Listen to another story. A certain man owned some land and planted a vineyard on it. He put up a wall around it, dug a pit for a winepress, and built a lookout tower. Then he rented the vineyard out to some farmers and moved to another place. When harvest time came, he sent his slaves to the renters to collect his share of the fruit.

"But the renters mistreated his slaves. They beat one of them, killed another, and threw stones at a third. Then the man sent a larger group of slaves to the renters, but they treated them the same way. So finally, he sent his son to them, thinking, 'They will respect my son.'

"But when the renters saw the son coming, they said to one another, 'He's supposed to inherit all the owner's property someday. Come on, let's kill him, and then everything will be ours.' So they grabbed him and dragged him out of the vineyard and killed him.

"What will the owner of the vineyard come and do to those renters?"

"He'll make those cruel men suffer a cruel death," they replied. "Then he'll rent the vineyard out to other renters who will give him his share of the crop at harvest time."

Jesus said to them, "Haven't you ever read this in the Scriptures? "'The stone the builders wouldn't accept has become the most important stone of all. The Lord has done this, and it's wonderful in our eyes.'

"So I tell you that the kingdom of God is going to be taken away from you and given to people who will produce its fruit. Anyone who falls on that stone will be broken to pieces, and the stone will crush anyone it falls on."

When the chief priests and the Pharisees heard Jesus' stories, they knew he was talking about them. They looked for a way to arrest him, but they were afraid of the crowd, because the people believed that Jesus was a prophet. Matt. 21:23-46

The Pharisees went out and made a plan to trap Jesus with his own words. They sent their disciples to him with some of the Herodians.

"Teacher," they said, "we know that you're a man of integrity and that you teach the way of God truthfully. You don't let others influence what you do or say, no matter how important they are. Tell us, then, what do you think? According to the law of Moses, should we pay the royal tax to Caesar?"

But Jesus knew they had bad motives for asking. He said, "You hypocrites! Why are you trying to trap me? Show me the coin people use for paying the tax."

They brought him a silver coin, and he asked them, "Whose picture is on this coin? And whose name and titles?"

"Caesar's," they replied.

Then he said to them, "So give to Caesar what belongs to Caesar, and give to God what belongs to God."

When they heard this, they were amazed. They left him and went away.

That same day the Sadducees, who don't believe that people rise from the dead, came to Jesus with a question.

"Teacher," they said, "Moses told us that if a man marries but dies without having children, his brother has to marry the widow so she can have children to carry on her late husband's name. There were seven brothers among us. The first one got married, but he died without having any children, so the next brother married his widow. But then the same thing happened to him, and to the third brother, right on down to the seventh brother. Finally, the woman died. Now then, when the dead rise, whose wife will she be? All seven brothers were married to her."

Jesus replied, "You're going wrong here because you don't know the Scriptures and you don't know the power of God. When the dead rise, people won't get married, and parents won't arrange marriages for their children. Everyone will be like the angels in heaven. But as for whether people rise from the dead, haven't you read what God said to you? 'I am the God of Abraham, the God of Isaac, and the God of Jacob.' He isn't the God of the dead; he's the God of the living."

When the crowds heard this, they were amazed by what Jesus taught.

The Pharisees heard that the Sadducees hadn't able to answer Jesus. So they got together, and one of them, an authority on the law, tested Jesus with a question. "Teacher," he asked, "which commandment in the Law is the greatest?"

Jesus answered, " 'Love the Lord your God with all your heart, with all your soul, and with all your mind.' That is the first and most important commandment. And the second is like it: 'Love your neighbor as you love yourself.' Everything written in the Law and the Prophets is based on these two commandments."

While the Pharisees were gathered together, Jesus asked them, "What do you think about the Messiah? Whose son is he?"

"The son of David," they replied.

He said to them, "Then why does David, speaking by the Spirit, call him 'Lord'? David said, "'The Lord said to my Lord, "Sit at my right hand until I put your enemies under your control."' So if David calls him 'Lord,' how can he be David's son?"

No one knew how to answer him, and from that day on, no one dared ask him any more questions. Matt. 22:15-46

Jesus said to the crowds and to his disciples, "The teachers of the law and the Pharisees base what they tell you on the teachings of Moses. So you must be careful to do everything they say. But don't do what they do, because they're all talk and no action. They tie up heavy, bulky loads and put them on other people's shoulders, but they aren't willing to lift a finger themselves to help.

"Everything they do is for others to see. People sometimes wear little boxes on their foreheads and arms that hold Scripture quotes. But they make their boxes big and obvious. People put tassels on the four corners of their clothes to remind them to obey God's commands. But they make their tassels extra long.

"They love to sit in the places of honor at dinners and have the most important seats in the synagogues. They love to be greeted with respect in the markets and to be called 'Rabbi.' But you shouldn't be called 'Rabbi,' because you have only one Teacher, and you are all brothers. And don't give anyone on earth the title 'father,' because you have only one Father, who is in heaven. And you shouldn't be called 'master,' because you have only one Master, and he's the Messiah. The greatest among you has to be your servant. People who lift themselves up will be humbled, but people who humble themselves will be lifted up.

"Woe to you, teachers of the law and Pharisees! You hypocrites! You shut the door of the kingdom of heaven in people's faces. You don't enter yourselves, but you won't let in other people who are trying to enter.

"Woe to you, teachers of the law and Pharisees! You hypocrites! You travel by land and sea to win one person to your way of living, but then you make them twice as much a child of hell as you are.

"Woe to you, blind guides! You say, 'If anyone makes a promise in the name of the temple, it means nothing. But if anyone makes a promise in the name of the gold in the temple, they have to keep that promise.' Blind fools! Which is greater: the gold, or the temple that makes the gold holy? You also say, 'If anyone makes a promise in the name of the altar, it means nothing. But if anyone makes a promise in the name of the gift on the altar, they have to keep that promise.' You're blind! Which is greater: the gift, or the altar that makes the gift holy? Any promise that's made in the name of the altar includes everything that's on it! In the same way, any promise that's made in the name of the temple includes the one who lives in it, and any promise made in the name of heaven includes God's throne and the one who sits on it.

"Woe to you, teachers of the law and Pharisees! You hypocrites! You give God a tenth of your spices like mint, dill, and cumin. But you've neglected the more important things in the law, which are justice, mercy, and faithfulness. You should have done those things and not neglected the first ones either. You blind guides! You strain a gnat out of your food, but then you swallow a whole camel!

"Woe to you, teachers of the law and Pharisees! You hypocrites! You clean the outside of the cup and dish, but the inside is full of greed and selfishness. Blind Pharisee! First clean the inside of the cup and dish, and then the outside will also be clean.

"Woe to you, teachers of the law and Pharisees! You hypocrites! You're like tombs that have been painted white. They look beautiful on the outside, but on the inside they're full of dead people's bones and other things that aren't pure and clean. You're just like that. On the outside you appear to be doing what's right, but on the inside you're full of hypocrisy and crime." Matt. 23:1-28

CHAPTER 16

TALKING ABOUT THE FUTURE

Jesus sat down across from the place where people gave their offerings at the temple. He watched as the crowd put their money into the offering boxes. Many rich people threw in large amounts. But a poor widow came along and put in two very small copper coins that were worth only a few pennies.

Jesus called over his disciples and said, "Truly I tell you, this poor widow has put more into the offering box than all the others. They gave a lot of money, but it was extra money they could afford to give. She gave even though she was poor. She put in all she had—everything she needed to live on." Mark 12:41-44

As Jesus was leaving the temple, one of his disciples said to him, "Look, Teacher! What giant stones! What wonderful buildings!"

"Do you see these huge buildings?" Jesus asked. "Not one stone here will be left on top of another. Every stone will be thrown down to the ground."

As Jesus was sitting on the Mount of Olives, across from the temple, Peter, James, John, and Andrew asked him privately, "Tell us, when will these things happen? And what will be the sign that they are all about to take place?"

Jesus told them, "Watch out so no one tricks you. Many people will come claiming to be me and saying, 'I'm the Messiah!' They'll get many people to follow them. You'll hear about wars, and you'll hear people saying there are going to be wars. Don't be afraid. Those things will happen, but that won't be the end. Nation will fight against nation, and kingdom will fight against kingdom. People won't have enough food, and there will be earthquakes in many places. But all of this will be only the beginning of the birth pains.

"Look out—you'll be handed over to the local courts, and you'll be whipped in the synagogues. You'll be brought in for questioning by governors and kings because of me. But in that way, you'll become witnesses to them. The good news has to be preached to all nations first. You'll be arrested and put on trial. But don't worry ahead of time about what to say. Just say what God brings to your mind at the time. It won't be you speaking; it will be the Holy Spirit.

"Brothers will hand over their brothers to be killed, and fathers will hand over their children. Children will rebel against their parents and have them put to death. Everyone will hate you because of me. But the one who stands firm to the end will be saved. Mark 13:1-13

"A time is coming when you will see armies surround Jerusalem. Then you will know that it will soon be destroyed. Those who are in Judea should then escape to the mountains. Those who are in the city should get out, and those who are in the country should not enter the city. This is the time when God will punish Jerusalem. Everything will come true, just as it has been written. How awful it will be in those days for pregnant women and for nursing mothers! There will be terrible suffering in the land and great anger against its people. Some will be killed by the sword and others will be taken as prisoners to all the nations. Jerusalem will be taken over by Gentiles until the times of the Gentiles come to an end.

"There will be signs in the sun, moon, and stars. The nations of the earth will be distressed and confused by the roaring and tossing of the sea. People will faint from terror because they are so worried about what is happening in the world. The sun, moon, and stars will be shaken from their places. At that time people will see the Son of Man coming in a cloud with power and great glory. When these things begin to happen, stand up and hold your heads high, because the time is near when you will be set free."

Jesus told them a story. "Look at the fig tree and all the trees," he said. "When you see leaves appear on the branches, you know that summer is near. In the same way, when you see these things happening, you will know that God's kingdom is near.

"Truly I tell you, this generation will not pass away until all these things have happened. Heaven and earth will pass away, but my words will never pass away.

"Be careful, or your hearts will be loaded down with partying, drunkenness, and the worries of life. Then the day when the Son of Man returns will close on you suddenly like a trap. That day will come on every person who lives on the whole earth. So always keep watching. Pray that you will be able to escape all that is about to happen, and pray that you will be able to stand before the Son of Man. Luke 21:20-36

"Be dressed and ready to serve and keep your lamps burning, like servants who are waiting for their master to return from a wedding dinner so that when he comes and knocks, they can open the door for him right away. Truly I tell you, if that master finds his servants watching for him when he comes, he'll do something special for them. He'll dress to serve them, have them take their places at the table, and come and wait on them. It will be good for those servants whose master finds them ready, especially if the master comes in the middle of the night or near dawn. But understand this: If the owner of a house knew when a burglar was coming, he wouldn't let him break into his house. You have to be ready too, because the Son of Man is going to come at a time when you're not expecting him."

Peter asked, "Lord, are you telling this story to us, or to everyone?"

The Lord answered, "Suppose a master gives one of his servants the job of giving the other servants their food at the right time, as a faithful and wise manager. It will be good for that servant if the master finds him doing this job when he returns. Truly I tell you, the master will put him in charge of everything he owns. But suppose the servant says to himself, 'My master is taking a long time to come back,' and he begins to beat the other servants. Suppose that instead of feeding those men and women, he only feeds himself and drinks until he gets drunk. His master will come back on a day and at a time when he isn't expecting him, and he will cut him to pieces and assign him a place with the unbelievers.

"If a servant knows his master's wishes but doesn't get ready and doesn't do what the master wants, he will receive a heavy beating. But if a servant doesn't know the master's wishes and does things for which he should be punished, he will receive a lighter beating. If someone has been given a lot, a lot will be expected of him; more will be asked of the person who has been entrusted with many responsibilities. Luke 12:35-48

"This is what the kingdom of heaven will be like at that time. Ten bridesmaids took their lamps and went outside the bride's house to wait for the groom to come and get her. Five of the bridesmaids were foolish and five were wise. The foolish ones took their lamps, but they didn't take any olive oil with them. The wise ones brought oil in jars along with their lamps. The groom was expected that evening, but when he didn't come for a long time, all the bridesmaids grew tired and fell asleep.

"At midnight someone cried out, 'The groom is coming! Go out and meet him!'

"Then all the bridesmaids woke up and got their lamps ready. The foolish ones said to the wise ones, 'Give us some of your oil, because our lamps are going out.'

" 'No,' they answered, 'because there might not be enough for all of us. Go to those who sell oil and buy some for yourselves.'

"So they went off to buy oil, and while they were away, the groom arrived. The bridesmaids who were ready went in with him to the wedding dinner. Then the door was shut.

"When the other bridesmaids got back, they called out, 'Master! Master! Open the door for us!'

"But the groom replied, 'Truly I tell you, I don't know you.'

"So keep watch. You don't know the day or the hour when the groom will arrive. Matt. 25:1-13

"When the Son of Man comes in his glory and all the angels come with him, he will sit on his glorious throne and all the nations will be gathered in front of him. He will separate the people into two groups, the way a shepherd separates the sheep from the goats. He'll put the sheep on his right and the goats on his left.

"Then the King will speak to those on his right and say, 'Come, you who are blessed by my Father, take what is yours. Receive the kingdom that has been prepared for you since the world was created. When I was hungry, you gave me something to eat, and when I was thirsty, you gave me something to drink. I was a stranger, and you welcomed me; I needed clothes, and you gave some to me. I was sick, and you took care of me; I was in prison, and you came to visit me.'

"Then the people who did what was right will answer him, 'Lord, when did we see you hungry and feed you, or thirsty and give you something to drink? When did we welcome you when you were a stranger? When did we see that you needed clothes and give some to you? When did we see that you were sick or in prison and come to visit you?'

"The King will reply, 'Truly I tell you, whatever you did for one of the least of these brothers and sisters of mine, you did for me.'

"Then he will say to those on his left, 'Go away from me, you who are cursed, into the fire that burns forever that has been prepared for the devil and his angels! I was hungry, but you didn't give me anything to eat. I was thirsty, but you didn't give me anything to drink. I was a stranger, but you didn't welcome me. I needed clothes, but you didn't give me any. I was sick and in prison, but you didn't take care of me.'

"They also will answer, 'Lord, when did we see you hungry or thirsty and not help you? When did we see that you were a stranger, or that you needed clothes, or that you were sick or in prison, and not help you?'

"He will reply, 'Truly I tell you, whatever you failed to do for one of the least of these brothers and sisters of mine, you failed to do for me.'

"Then they will go away to be punished forever, but those who did what was right will receive eternal life." Matt. 25:31-46

When the Passover and the Feast of Unleavened Bread were only two days away, the chief priests and the teachers of the law got together to make plans to arrest Jesus secretly and kill him. "But we can't do it during the feast," they agreed, "or the people may riot."

Jesus was in Bethany, eating dinner in the home of Simon the Leper. A woman came in with an alabaster jar that contained very expensive perfume made out of pure nard. She broke the jar open and poured the perfume on Jesus' head.

Some of the people there got angry and said to one another, "Why did she waste that perfume? It could have been sold for more than a year's pay, and the money could have been given to the poor." And they started angrily telling the woman that she'd done something wrong.

"Leave her alone," Jesus told them. "Why are you criticizing her? She has done a beautiful thing for me. You'll always have the poor with you, and you can help them any time you want. But you won't always have me. She did what she could. She poured perfume on my body to prepare me for burial. Truly I tell you, what she has done will be told wherever the good news is preached all over the world, and she will be remembered." Mark 14:1-9

The Pharisee who had invited Jesus saw this. He said to himself, "If this man were a prophet, he would know who is touching him—what kind of woman she is. She's a sinner!"

Jesus responded, "Simon, I have something to tell you."

"Tell me, teacher," he said.

"Two people owed money to a certain lender. One of them owed him 500 silver coins, while the other owed 50 silver coins. Neither of them had the money to pay him back, so he told them both they didn't have to pay. Which of them will love him more?"

Simon replied, "I suppose the one who owed the most money."

"You're right," Jesus said.

Then he turned toward the woman and said to Simon, "Do you see this woman? When I came into your house, you didn't give me any water to wash my feet, but she has wet my feet with her tears and wiped them with her hair. You didn't give me a kiss, but this woman hasn't stopped kissing my feet since I came in. You didn't put any olive oil on my head, but she has poured this perfume on my feet. So I tell you this: Her many sins have been forgiven, as her acts of great love have shown. But whoever has been forgiven only a little loves only a little."

Then Jesus said to her, "Your sins are forgiven."

The other guests began to ask each other, "Who is this who even forgives sins?"

Jesus said to the woman, "Your faith has saved you. Go in peace." Luke 7:39-50

Meanwhile a large crowd of Jews found out that Jesus was there in Bethany. They came out not just to see him but also to see Lazarus, the man Jesus had raised from the dead. So the chief priests made plans to kill Lazarus too, since many of the Jews were starting to follow and believe in Jesus because of him. John 12:9-11

CHAPTER 17

BETRAYED BY A FRIEND

The Feast of Unleavened Bread, called the Passover, was near. The chief priests and the teachers of the law were looking for a way to get rid of Jesus, because they were afraid of the people. Then Satan entered into Judas, who was called Iscariot. He was one of the 12 disciples. He went to the chief priests and the officers of the temple guard and talked with them about how he could hand Jesus over to them. They were delighted and agreed to give him money. Judas accepted their offer and began to watch for a time to hand Jesus over to them when no crowd was around.

Then the day of Unleavened Bread came, when the Passover lamb had to be sacrificed. Jesus sent Peter and John on ahead and told them, "Go, prepare for us to eat the Passover meal."

"Where do you want us to prepare for it?" they asked.

Jesus replied, "When you enter the city, a man carrying a jar of water will meet you. Follow him to the house that he enters and say to the owner of the house, 'The Teacher asks, "Where is the guest room where I can eat the Passover meal with my disciples?"' He will show you a large upstairs room with furniture already in it. Prepare for us to eat there."

Peter and John left, and they found things just as Jesus had told them. So they prepared the Passover meal.

When the time came, Jesus and his apostles took their places at the table. He said to them, "I have really looked forward to eating this Passover meal with you. I wanted to do this before I suffered. I tell you, I will not eat the Passover meal again until it is celebrated in God's kingdom." Luke 22:1-16

Jesus knew that the time had come for him to leave this world and go to the Father. Jesus had always loved his disciples who were in the world, and he now loved them to the very end.

They were having their evening meal. The devil had already put in the mind of Judas, the son of Simon Iscariot, the scheme of handing Jesus over to his enemies. Jesus knew that the Father had put everything under his power, and that he had come from God and was returning to God. So he got up from the meal, took off his outer clothes, and wrapped a towel around his waist. After that, he poured water into a large bowl and began to wash his disciples' feet. He dried them with the towel that was wrapped around him.

When he got to Simon Peter, Peter said, "Lord, are you going to wash my feet?"

Jesus answered, "You don't realize now what I am doing, but later you will understand."

"No," said Peter, "I'll never let you wash my feet."

Jesus responded, "Unless I wash them, you can't be part of what I'm doing."

"Then not just my feet, Lord," Simon Peter replied. "Wash my hands and my head too!"

Jesus answered, "People who've had a bath only need to wash their feet. The rest of their body is clean. And you are clean—but not all of you are." Jesus knew who was going to hand him over to his enemies. That was why he said not every one of them was clean.

When Jesus had finished washing their feet, he put his clothes back on and returned to his place. "Do you understand what I've done for you?" he asked them. "You call me 'Teacher' and 'Lord,' and that's the right thing to do, because that's what I am. If I, your Lord and Teacher, have washed your feet, you should also wash one another's feet. I've given you an example. You should do as I have done for you. Truly I tell you, a slave is not greater than his master. A messenger isn't greater than the one who sends him. Now that you know these things, you'll be blessed if you do them.

"I'm not talking about all of you. I know the ones I've chosen. But something is going to happen to make the passage of Scripture come true that says, 'The one who shared my bread has turned against me.'

"I'm telling you this now, before it happens, so that when it does happen, you'll believe that I am who I am. Truly I tell you, whoever accepts anyone I send accepts me, and whoever who accepts me accepts the one who sent me." John 13:1-20

Jesus took the cup and gave thanks. He said, "Take this cup and share it among yourselves. I tell you, I will not drink wine with you again until God's kingdom comes."

Then Jesus took bread. He gave thanks, broke it, gave it to them, and said, "This is my body, given for you; do this in memory of me."

In the same way, after the supper he took the cup and said, "This cup is the new covenant in my blood, which is poured out for you. Luke 22:17-20

After he'd said this, Jesus became distressed and said, "Truly I tell you, one of you is going to hand me over to my enemies."

His disciples looked at one another. They didn't have any idea which one of them he meant. The disciple Jesus loved [John] was next to him at the table. Simon Peter motioned to that disciple and said to him, "Ask Jesus which one he means."

The disciple leaned back against Jesus and asked him, "Lord, who is it?"

Jesus answered, "It's the one I'll give this piece of bread to after I've dipped it in the dish."

He dipped the bread in the dish and gave it to Judas, the son of Simon Iscariot. As soon as Judas took the bread, Satan entered into him.

So Jesus told him, "Do quickly what you're going to do." But no one at the meal understood why Jesus said this to him. Since Judas was in charge of the money, some of the disciples thought Jesus was telling him to buy what was needed for the feast. Others thought Jesus was talking about giving something to the poor.

As soon as Judas had taken the bread, he went out. And it was night.

After Judas was gone, Jesus said, "Now the Son of Man is going to receive glory and bring glory to God. If the Son brings glory to God, God himself will bring glory to the Son, and God will do it right away. "My children, I will be with you only a little while longer. You will look for me, and just as I told the Jews, so I am telling you now: You can't come where I'm going.

"I'm giving you a new command: Love one another. You must love one another just as I have loved you. If you do love one another, then everyone will know that you are my disciples." John 13:21-35

Then they sang a hymn, and they went out to the Mount of Olives.

Jesus told them, "You're all going to abandon me this very night. It's written that the Lord said," 'I will strike the shepherd down, and then the sheep of the flock will be scattered.' But after I rise from the dead, I will go ahead of you into Galilee."

Peter replied, "Even if all the others abandon you, I never will."

"Truly I tell you," Jesus answered, "this very night, before the rooster crows, you'll claim three times that you don't know me."

But Peter insisted, "Even if I have to die with you, I'll never say that I don't know you."

And all the other disciples said the same thing. Matt. 26:30-35

Then Jesus asked the disciples, "Did you lack anything when I sent you without a purse, bag, or sandals?"

"Nothing," they answered.

He said to them, "But now if you do have a purse, take it. And also take a bag. If you don't have a sword, sell your coat and buy one. It is written, 'He was counted among those who had committed crimes.' I tell you that what is written about me must come true. In fact, it is already coming true."

The disciples said, "See, Lord, here are two swords."

"Two swords are enough," he replied. Luke 22:35-38

"Don't let your hearts be troubled. You believe in God; believe in me too. There are many rooms in my Father's house. If there weren't, would I have told you that I'm going there to prepare a place for you? And after I go and prepare a place for you, I'll come back and take you to be with me. That way you'll also be where I am. You know the way to the place where I'm going."

Thomas said to him, "Lord, we don't know where you're going. So how can we know the way?"

Jesus answered, "I am the way and the truth and the life. No one comes to the Father except through me. If you really know me, you will know my Father also. From now on, you do know him and you've seen him."

Philip said, "Lord, show us the Father, and that will be enough for us."

Jesus answered, "Don't you know me, Philip, even after I've been with you for so long? Anyone who has seen me has seen the Father. So how can you say, 'Show us the Father'? Don't you believe that I am in the Father and the Father is in me? Whenever I speak to you, I'm not saying those words on my own authority. Rather, the Father who lives in me is doing his work. Believe me when I say that I am in the Father and the Father is in me. Or at least believe what the works I've been doing say about me. Truly I tell you, anyone who believes in me will do the works that I've been doing. In fact, they'll do even greater things, because I'm going to the Father. And I will do whatever you ask in my name, so that the Father may be glorified in the Son. If you ask me for anything in my name, I will do it.

"If you love me, obey my commands. And I will ask the Father, and he will give you another helper who will be with you forever. That helper is the Spirit of truth. The world can't accept him because it doesn't see him or know him. But you know him because he lives with you and will be in you. I will not leave you like children who don't have any parents. I will come to you. Before long, the world won't see me anymore, but you'll see me. Because I live, you too will live. On that day you'll realize that I am in my Father, and you are in me, and I am in you. Anyone who has my commands and obeys them loves me. My Father will love the one who loves me, and I too will love them and show myself to them."

Then another disciple said, "Lord why do you plan to show yourself to us but not to the world?"

Jesus answered, "Anyone who loves me will obey my teaching. My Father will love them, and we will come to them and make our home with them. Anyone who doesn't love me will not obey my teaching. The words you hear me saying aren't my own. They belong to the Father who sent me.

"I've spoken all these things while I'm still with you. But the Father will send the Helper, the Holy Spirit, in my name to help you. The Spirit will teach you all things and remind you of everything I've said to you.

"Peace I leave with you; I give my peace to you. I don't give to you the way the world does. So don't let your hearts be distressed, and don't be afraid. "You heard me say, 'I'm going away and I'm coming back to you.' If you loved me, you'd be glad that I'm going to the Father, because the Father is greater than I am. I've told you now before it happens, so that when it does happen, you'll believe. I won't say much more to you, because the prince of this world is coming. He has no power over me, but he's coming so that the world may learn that I love the Father and that I do exactly what my Father has commanded me to do. John 14:1-31

"I am the true vine, and my Father is the gardener. He cuts off any of my branches that don't bear fruit, and he trims every branch that does bear fruit so that it will bear even more fruit. You are already trimmed and clean because of the word I've spoken to you. Remain in me, just as I also remain in you. No branch can bear fruit by itself. It has to remain attached to the vine. In the same way, you can't bear fruit unless you remain in me.

"I remain in you, you will bear much fruit. Apart from me, you can do nothing. If you don't remain in me, you'll be like a branch that breaks off and dries up. Branches like that are picked up, thrown into the fire, and burned. But if you remain in me and my words remain in you, you can ask for anything you wish, and it will be done for you. It brings glory to my Father and shows that you're my disciples when you bear much fruit.

"Just as the Father has loved me, I have loved you. Now remain in my love. If you obey my commands, you will remain in my love. In the same way, I have obeyed my Father's commands and I remain in his love. I've told you this so that you'll have the same joy that I have and your joy will be complete.

"Here is my command: Love one another, just as I have loved you. The greatest love that anyone can show is to give up their life for their friends. You are my friends if you do what I command. I don't call you slaves anymore, because slaves don't know their master's plans. Instead, I've called you friends, because I've told you every-thing I've learned from my Father. You didn't choose me, I chose you. And I appointed you to go and bear fruit that would endure, so that you would receive from the Father anything you ask for in my name. Here is my command: Love one another.

"If the world hates you, remember that it hated me first. If you belonged to the world, it would love you as one of its own. But you don't belong to the world. I've chosen you out of the world. That's why the world hates you. Remember what I told you: 'A slave is not greater than his master.' If people have hated me and tried to hurt me, they will do the same to you. If they have obeyed my teaching, they will obey yours too. They will treat you as they do because of my name, because they don't know the one who sent me. If I hadn't come and spoken to them, they wouldn't be guilty of sin. But now they have no excuse for their sin. Whoever hates me hates my Father too. If I hadn't done works among them that no one else had done, they wouldn't be guilty of sin. But now they've seen those works and they've still hated both me and my Father. This has happened to make what's written in their Law come true. It says, 'They hated me without any reason.' John 15:1-25

"I've told you all this so that you won't turn away from the truth. You're going to be thrown out of the synagogue. In fact, the time is coming when anyone who kills you will think they're serving God. They'll do things like that because they don't know the Father and they don't know me. I've told you this so that when their time comes, you'll remember that I warned you about them.

"I didn't tell you this from the beginning because I was with you. But now I'm going to the one who sent me. None of you is asking me, 'Where are you going?' Instead, you're filled with sadness because I've said these things. But truly I tell you, it's for your good that I'm going away. Unless I go away, the Helper won't come to help you. But if I do go, I'll send him to you. When he comes, he will show the people of this world that they're guilty of sin, that they can be made right with God, and that if they aren't, they'll face judgment. They're guilty of sin because they don't believe in me. They can be made right with God because I'm going to the Father and you won't see me anymore. They're going to have to face judgment because the devil, the prince of this world, has already been judged.

"I have much more to say to you, but it's more than you can handle right now. But when the Spirit of truth comes, he'll guide you into all the truth. He won't speak on his own, he'll speak only what he hears. He'll tell you what's still going to happen. He will bring me glory because he'll take what I give him and show it to you. Everything that belongs to the Father is mine. That's why I said the Holy Spirit would receive from me the things that he will show you."

Jesus continued, "In a little while you won't see me anymore. Then after a little while you'll see me again."

When they heard this, some of his disciples asked one another, "What does he mean when he says, 'In a little while you won't see me anymore. Then after a little while you'll see me again'? And what does he mean when he says, 'I'm going to the Father'?" They kept asking, "What does he mean by 'a little while'? We don't understand what he's saying."

Jesus saw that they wanted to ask him about these things, so he said to them, "Are you asking each other what I meant when I said, 'In a little while you won't see me anymore, then after a little while you'll see me again'? Truly I tell you, you're going to weep and mourn while the world is full of joy. You'll be sad, but your sadness will turn into joy. A woman who's giving birth is in pain because she's in labor. But when her baby is born, she forgets about the pain because she's so happy that a baby has been born into the world. That's the way it will be with you. Now is a time of sadness for you, but I will see you again. Then you'll be full of joy, and no one will take your joy away.

"When that time comes, you won't ask me anything anymore. Truly I tell you, my Father will give you anything you ask for in my name. Up till now you haven't asked for anything in my name. Ask and you will receive, so that your joy will be complete.

"I've been telling you things using images and stories. But a time is coming when I won't use examples; I'll tell you plainly about my Father. When that day comes, you will ask for things in my name. I'm not saying that I will ask the Father instead of you asking him. No, the Father himself loves you because you have loved me and have believed that I came from God. I came from the Father and entered the world. Now I'm leaving the world and going back to the Father."

Then Jesus' disciples said, "Now you're speaking plainly and not using images and stories. Now we can see that you know everything and that you don't need anyone to ask you any questions. This makes us believe that you came from God."

"Do you believe now?" Jesus replied. "A time is coming when you'll be scattered and you'll go to your own homes. In fact, that time is already here. You'll leave me all alone. But I'm not really alone, because my Father is with me.

"I've told you these things so that you can have peace because of me. In this world you're going to have trouble. But be encouraged! I've already defeated the world." John 16:1-33

After Jesus said this, he looked toward heaven and prayed, "Father, the time has come. Bring glory to your Son so that your Son may bring glory to you. You've given him authority over all people so that he can give eternal life to all those you've given him. And this is eternal life: to know you, the only true God, and Jesus Christ, the one you've sent. I've brought you glory on earth by finishing the work you gave me to do. So now, Father, give me glory there with you, the glory I had with you before the world began.

"I have revealed your name to the disciples you gave me out of the world. They were yours; you gave them to me, and they have obeyed your word. Now they know that everything you've given me comes from you. I gave them the words you gave me, and they accepted them. They knew for certain that I came from you, and they believed that you sent me.

"I pray for them. I'm not praying for the world, but for those you've given me, because they're yours. All I have is yours, and all you have is mine. Glory has come to me because of my disciples. I'm not going to remain in the world any longer. But they are still in the world, and I'm coming to you. Holy Father, keep them safe by the power of your name, the name you gave me, so that they can be one just as you and I are one. While I was with them, I protected them and kept them safe through the name you gave me. Not one of them has been lost, except the one headed for destruction, so that Scripture would come true.

"I'm coming to you now, but I say these things while I'm still in the world so that those you gave me can have the same joy that I have. I've given them your word, and the world has hated them because they're not part of the world any more than I am. I'm not asking for you to take them out of the world. I'm asking for you to keep them safe from the evil one. They don't belong to the world, just as I don't belong to it. Set them apart, making them holy by the truth; your word is truth. Just as you sent me into the world, I've sent them into the world. I'm making myself holy for them so that they too can be made holy by the truth.

"I'm not praying only for them, I'm also praying for everyone who will believe in me through their message. Father, I pray they will be one, just as you are in me and I am in you. I want them also to be in us so that the world will believe that you have sent me. I've given them the glory you gave me so that they may be one, just as we are one. I will be in them, just as you are in me, so that they may be brought together perfectly as one. Then the world will know that you sent me and that you have loved them just as you have loved me.

"Father, I want those you've given me to be with me where I am. I want them to see my glory, the glory you have given me because you loved me before the world was created.

"Righteous Father, the world doesn't know you, but I know you, and they know you've sent me. I've made your name known to them, and I will continue to show you to them. Then the love you have for me will be in them, and I myself will be in them." John 17:1-26

They went to a place called Gethsemane, and Jesus told his disciples, "Sit here while I go pray." He took Peter, James, and John along with him. He became very distressed, and he said to them, "My soul is filled with anguish, and I feel like I might die. Stay here and keep watch."

He went a little farther, and then he fell to the ground and prayed that, if possible, he wouldn't have to go through the time that was coming. "*Abba*, Father," he said, "everything is possible for you. Take this cup of suffering away from me. Not what I want, though. Do what you want." Mark 14:32-36

An angel from heaven appeared to Jesus and gave him strength. Because he was so distressed, he prayed even harder, and his sweat became like drops of blood falling to the ground. Luke 22:43-44

Then he returned to his disciples and found them sleeping. "Couldn't any of you keep watch with me for one hour?" he asked Peter. "Watch and pray so that you won't fall into sin when you're tempted. The spirit is willing, but the body is weak."

Jesus went away a second time and prayed, "My Father, if it isn't possible for this cup to be taken away unless I drink it, then may your will be done."

Then he came back and found the three of them sleeping again. They couldn't keep their eyes open, so he left them and went off once more. He prayed the same thing a third time.

Then he returned to the disciples and said to them, "Are you still sleeping and resting? Look! The time has come. The Son of Man is about to be handed over to sinners. Get up! Let's go! Here comes the one who's handing me over to them!"

While Jesus was still speaking, Judas, who was one of the 12 disciples, arrived. He had a group of men with him who were carrying swords and clubs. The chief priests and elders of the people had sent them.

Judas had arranged to hand Jesus over by giving them a signal. "The one I kiss will be the man," he'd told them, "Arrest him!" Judas went right over to Jesus and said, "Greetings, Rabbi!" Then he kissed him. Matt. 26:40-49

But Jesus asked him, "Judas, are you handing over the Son of Man with a kiss?"

Jesus' followers saw what was going to happen and they asked, "Lord, should we use our swords against them?" One of them [Peter] struck the slave of the high priest and cut off his right ear.

But Jesus answered, "Stop this!" And he touched the man's ear and healed him.

Then Jesus said to the chief priests, the officers of the temple guard, and the elders, who had come for him, "Am I leading a band of armed men against you? Did you have to come with swords and clubs? Every day I was with you in the temple courtyard, yet you didn't lay a hand on me. But this is your time, when darkness rules." Luke 22:48-53

Then all his disciples abandoned him and ran away. A young man [by tradition Mark] was following Jesus, wearing just a linen cloth. The men tried to grab him too, but he wriggled out of his clothing and ran away naked. Mark 14:50-52

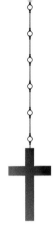

CHAPTER 18

FACING FALSE CHARGES

Those who had arrested Jesus took him to Caiaphas, the high priest. The teachers of the law and the elders had already gathered in his palace. Peter had followed Jesus from a distance, and now he came as close as the courtyard. He went in and sat down with the guards to see what would happen.

The chief priests and the whole council of elders, called the Sanhedrin, were looking for false evidence against Jesus so that they could put him to death. But they couldn't find anything to use, even though many false witnesses came forward.

Finally, two witnesses came forward and testified, "This man said, 'I'm able to destroy the temple of God and rebuild it in three days.'"

Then the high priest stood up to question Jesus. "Aren't you going to answer?" he asked. "What have you got to say to the charges these men are bringing against you?" But Jesus remained silent.

The high priest said to him, "Tell us, under oath to the living God, whether you are the Messiah, the Son of God."

"You have said so," Jesus replied. "But I say to all of you that after this you will see the Son of Man sitting at the right hand of the Mighty One, coming on the clouds of heaven."

Then the high priest ripped his clothes and said, "This man has claimed to be God! Why do we need any more witnesses? You've heard what he said. What do you think?"

"He must die!" they answered.

Then they spit in his face and hit him with their fists. Others slapped him and said, "Prophesy to us, Messiah! Who hit you?"

Meanwhile, Peter was sitting out in the courtyard. A female servant came up to him and said, "You also were with Jesus of Galilee."

But Peter denied it in front of everyone. "I don't know what you're talking about," he insisted.

Then he moved out to the gate that led into the courtyard. There another servant saw him and said to the people, "This man was with Jesus of Nazareth."

Again he denied it and said, "I swear I don't know the man!"

After a little while, the people standing there came up to Peter and said, "You must be one of them. Your accent gives you away."

"I swear that I don't know the man!" Peter said again. "May I be cursed if I'm not telling the truth!"

Just then a rooster crowed. Peter remembered that Jesus had said, "Before the rooster crows, you will deny me three times." Peter went outside and wept bitterly. Matt. 26:57-75

Early in the morning, all the chief priests and elders of the people met to plan how to put Jesus to death. They tied him up, took him away, and turned him over to Pilate, the governor.

When Judas, who had betrayed him, saw that Jesus had been sentenced to die, he felt deep shame and sadness for what he'd done. So he returned the 30 silver coins to the chief priests and the elders. "I've sinned," he told them. "I've handed over a man who isn't guilty."

"What do we care?" they answered. "That's your problem."

So Judas threw the money into the temple and left. Then he went away and hanged himself.

The chief priests picked up the coins and said, "It's against the law to put this money into the temple fund because it's blood money. It has paid for a man's death." So they decided to use the money to buy some land where foreigners could be buried. They chose the Potter's Field. Because it was bought with the "blood money," it has been called the Field of Blood ever since.

In this way the words of Jeremiah the prophet came true. He had said, "They took the 30 silver coins, which was how much the people of Israel thought he was worth, and they used the coins to buy a potter's field, just as the Lord commanded me." Matt. 27:1-10

Then the Jewish leaders took Jesus from Caiaphas to the palace of the Roman governor. By now it was early morning. The Jewish leaders didn't enter the palace, because they didn't want to be made unclean. They wanted to be able to eat the Passover meal. So Pilate came out to them. He asked, "What charges are you bringing against this man?"

"He's a criminal," they answered. "If he weren't, we wouldn't have handed him over to you."

Pilate said, "Take him yourselves and judge him by your own law."

"But we're not allowed to put anyone to death," they responded. This happened so that what Jesus had said about how he was going to die would come true. John 18:28-32

They began to make accusations against him. They said, "We've found this man leading our people astray. He says they shouldn't pay taxes to Caesar, and he claims to be the Messiah—a king." Luke 23:2

Then Pilate went back inside the palace and ordered Jesus to be brought to him. Pilate asked him, "Are you the king of the Jews?"

"Are you concerned about that yourself?" Jesus asked. "Or is that what others have been telling you about me?"

"Am I a Jew?" Pilate replied. "Your own people and chief priests have handed you over to me. What have you done?"

Jesus said, "My kingdom is not of this world. If it were, my servants would have fought to keep the Jewish leaders from arresting me. My kingdom is from another place."

"So you're a king, then!" said Pilate.

Jesus answered, "You say that I'm a king. The reason I was born and came into the world was to be a witness to the truth. Everyone who is on the side of truth listens to me."

"What is truth?" Pilate retorted.

Then he went out again to the Jews who were gathered there. He said, "I don't find any basis for a charge against him." John 18:33-38

But they insisted, "His teaching stirs up the people all over Judea. He started in Galilee and has come all the way here."

When Pilate heard this, he asked if the man was from Galilee. When he learned that Jesus came from Herod's area of authority, he sent Jesus over to Herod, who was also in Jerusalem at that time.

When Herod saw Jesus, he was very pleased, because he'd been wanting to see him for a long time. He'd heard much about him, and he hoped to see him perform some kind of sign. Herod asked Jesus many questions, but he gave no answer. The chief priests and the teachers of the law were standing there, shouting out accusations against him.

Herod and his soldiers mocked Jesus and made fun of him. They dressed him in a fancy robe and then sent him back to Pilate. That day Herod and Pilate became friends; they'd been enemies previously.

Pilate called together the chief priests, the rulers, and the people. He said to them, "You brought me this man and said he was turning the people against the authorities. I have questioned him in front of you, and I have found no basis for your charges against him. Herod didn't either—that's why he sent him back to us. As you can see, Jesus has done nothing worthy of death. So I will have him whipped and let him go." Luke 23:5-16

As soon as the chief priests and officials saw him, they shouted, "Crucify him! Crucify him!"

But Pilate answered, "You take him and crucify him. I haven't found any basis for a charge against him myself."

The Jewish leaders replied, "We have a law, and according to that law he must die, because he claimed to be the Son of God."

When Pilate heard that, he was even more afraid. He went back inside the palace and asked Jesus, "Where do you come from?" But Jesus didn't answer him.

"Are you refusing to speak to me?" Pilate said. "Don't you understand? I have the power to set you free or to nail you to a cross."

Jesus answered, "You wouldn't have any power over me if it hadn't been given to you from heaven. So the one who handed me over to you is guilty of a greater sin."

From then on, Pilate tried to set Jesus free. But the Jewish leaders kept shouting, "If you let this man go, you're not Caesar's friend! Anyone who claims to be a king is against Caesar!" John 19:6-12

Every year at the Passover Feast the governor would let one prisoner go free. The people could choose the one they wanted. At that time there was a notorious prisoner named Jesus Barabbas. So when the crowd gathered, Pilate asked them, "Which one do you want me to set free? Jesus Barabbas, or Jesus who's called the Messiah?" Pilate knew that the leaders had handed Jesus over because they were jealous.

Pilate also wanted to release Jesus because he'd gotten a message from his wife while he was judging the case. The message said, "Don't do anything to that man. He's innocent. I had a terrible nightmare about him last night."

But the chief priests and the elders talked the crowd into asking Pilate to set Barabbas free and put Jesus to death.

"Which of the two do you want me to set free?" asked the governor.

"Barabbas," they answered.

"Then what should I do with Jesus who is called the Messiah?" Pilate asked.

They all answered, "Crucify him!"

"Why? What wrong has he done?" asked Pilate.

But they shouted even more loudly, "Crucify him!"

Pilate saw that he wasn't getting anywhere. Instead, the crowd was starting to get angry. So he took water and washed his hands in front of them. "I'm not guilty of this man's death," he said. "You're accountable for that!"

All the people answered, "Put the blame for his death on us and our children!"

Then to make the people happy Pilate set Barabbas free. He had Jesus whipped, and then he handed him over to be crucified. Matt. 27:15-26

CHAPTER 19

NAILED TO A CROSS

The soldiers led Jesus away into the palace, which was called the Praetorium. There they called together the whole company of soldiers. They put a purple robe on Jesus, twisted thorns together to make a crown, and forced it onto his head. They pretended to greet him the way they would Caesar: "Hail, king of the Jews!" But then they repeatedly beat him on the head with a stick and spit on him. They fell on their knees and pretended to honor him.

After they had made fun of him, they took off the purple robe and put his own clothes back on him. Then they led him out to nail him to a cross.

A man from Cyrene named Simon (he's the father of Alexander and Rufus) was coming in from the country. When he went past the soldiers who were leading Jesus away, they stopped him and forced him to carry the cross. Mark 15:16-21

A large number of people followed Jesus, including women who mourned and cried aloud because of him. Jesus turned to them and said, "Daughters of Jerusalem, don't weep for me; weep for yourselves and for your children. A time is coming when you will say, 'Blessed are the women who couldn't have children! Blessed are those who never gave birth or nursed babies!' Then, as it is written, 'The people will say to the mountains, "Fall on us!" They'll say to the hills, "Cover us!"' If people do these things when the trees are green, what will they do when the trees are dry?"

Two other men were also led out with Jesus to be killed. Both of them had broken the law. The soldiers brought them all to the place called the Skull. There they nailed Jesus to the cross and did the same with the two criminals, one on his right and the other on his left.

Jesus said, "Father, forgive them, because they don't know what they're doing." Luke 23:27-34

Pilate had a notice prepared and fastened to the cross. It read, JESUS OF NAZARETH, THE KING OF THE JEWS.

Many of the Jews read the sign because the place where Jesus was crucified was near the city, and the sign was written in Hebrew, Latin, and Greek. The Jewish chief priests argued with Pilate and said, "You shouldn't have written, 'The King of the Jews.' Write that this man claimed he was king of the Jews."

Pilate answered, "What I have written, I have written."

When the soldiers crucified Jesus, they took his clothes and divided them into four parts, one share for each of them. All that was left was Jesus' long, inner robe. It didn't have any seams; it was made out of one piece of cloth from top to bottom. "Let's not tear it in pieces," they said to one another. "Let's cast lots to see who will take it." This happened so that the Scripture would come true that says, "They divided up my clothes among them, and they cast lots for what I was wearing." So that's what the soldiers did. John 19:19-24

People who were passing by shouted insults at Jesus and made fun of him. They shook their heads and said, "So, you're going to destroy the temple and build it again in three days? Then save yourself! Come down from the cross, if you're the Son of God!"

In the same way the chief priests, teachers of the law, and elders made fun of him. "He saved others," they said, "but he can't save himself! He's supposed to be the king of Israel. Let him come down from that cross, and we'll believe in him! He trusts in God; let God rescue him now, if he's so pleased with him. After all, he said, 'I'm the Son of God.' " Matt. 27:39-43

One of the criminals who was hanging there made fun of Jesus. "Aren't you the Messiah?" he asked. "Save yourself and save us!"

But the other criminal corrected him. "Don't you have any respect for God?" he asked. "Remember, you're under the same death sentence. We're being punished fairly and getting what our actions deserve. But this man hasn't done anything wrong."

Then he said, "Jesus, remember me when you come into your kingdom."

Jesus answered him, "Truly I tell you, today you will be with me in paradise." Luke 23:39-43

Jesus' mother was standing near his cross, as was his mother's sister, Mary the wife of Clopas, and Mary Magdalene. When Jesus saw his mother there, and the disciple he loved standing nearby, he said to his mother, "Dear woman, this is your son." And he said to the disciple, "This is your mother." From that time on, the disciple took her into his home. John 19:25-27

From noon until three o'clock, the whole land was covered with darkness. At about three o'clock, Jesus cried out in a loud voice, "*Eli, Eli, lema sabachthani?*" (That means, "My God, my God, why have you abandoned me?")

When some of those who were standing there heard Jesus cry out, they said, "He's calling for Elijah!" Matt. 27:45-47

When Jesus knew that everything had now been finished, so that Scripture would come true, he said, "I'm thirsty." A jar of wine vinegar was there, so they soaked a sponge in it, put the sponge on the stem of a hyssop plant, and lifted it up to Jesus' lips. After Jesus drank it, he said, "It is finished."

Then he bowed his head and died. John 19:28-30

At that moment the curtain in front of the Most Holy Place in the temple was torn in half from top to bottom. The earth shook, the rocks split, and tombs broke open. The bodies of many holy people who had died were raised to life. They came out of their tombs after Jesus was raised from the dead, and they went into the holy city and appeared to many people there.

When the Roman commander and those who were guarding Jesus saw the earthquake and everything that had happened, they were terrified and exclaimed, "He had to be the Son of God!"

Many women were watching from a distance. They had followed Jesus from Galilee to take care of his needs. Among them were Mary Magdalene, Mary the mother of James and Joseph, and the mother of Zebedee's sons. Matt. 27:51-56

It was Preparation Day. The next day would be a special Sabbath day. The Jewish leaders didn't want the bodies to be left on the crosses during the Sabbath day, so they asked Pilate to have the men's legs broken and their bodies taken down.

The soldiers came and broke the legs of the first man who'd been crucified with Jesus. Then they broke the legs of the other man. But when they came to Jesus, they saw that he was already dead. So they didn't break his legs. Instead, one of the soldiers stuck his spear into Jesus' side, and right away blood and water flowed out.

The man who saw this [John] has now given his testimony about it, and what he has to say is true. He knows that he's telling the truth, and he's giving his testimony so that you too may believe. These things happened to make the Scripture come true that says, "Not one of his bones will be broken." They also made the Scripture come true that says, "They will look at the one they have pierced."

Afterwards, Joseph of Arimathea asked Pilate for Jesus' body. Joseph was a follower of Jesus, but secretly, because he was afraid of the Jewish leaders. With Pilate's permission, Joseph came and took

NAILED TO A CROSS

the body away. Nicodemus, the man who earlier had visited Jesus at night, came with him. Nicodemus brought a mixture of spices that weighed about 75 pounds. John 19:31-39 Joseph took the body and wrapped it in a clean linen cloth, and then he placed it in his own new tomb, which had been carved out of the rock. He rolled a big stone in front of the entrance to the tomb and then went away. But Mary Magdalene and the other Mary stayed there a while longer, sitting opposite the tomb.

The next day, which was the Sabbath day, the chief priests and the Pharisees went to Pilate. "Sir," they said, "we remember something that this liar said while he was still alive. He claimed, 'After three days I will rise again.' So give an order to make the tomb secure until the third day. If you don't, his disciples might come and steal his body. Then they'll tell the people that Jesus has risen from the dead, and that last lie will be worse than the first."

"Take some guards," Pilate answered, "and go and make the tomb as secure as you can."

So they went and made the tomb secure by putting a royal seal on the stone and posting guards on duty. Matt. 27:59-66

CHAPTER 20

BACK FROM THE DEAD

When the Sabbath day was over, Mary Magdalene, Mary the mother of James, and Salome bought spices to put on Jesus' body. They went to the tomb very early on the first day of the week, just after sunrise.

On the way they were asking each other, "Who will roll the stone away from the entrance to the tomb?" But as they approached, they could see that the stone, even though it was very large, had already been rolled away.

When they went into the tomb, they saw a young man dressed in a white robe sitting on the right side, and they were distressed.

"Don't be distressed," he said. "You're looking for Jesus the Nazarene, who was crucified. He's not here! He has risen! Look, this is where his body was. Mark 16:1-6 Remember how he told you while he was still with you in Galilee that he would rise? He said, 'The Son of Man must be handed over to sinful people and be nailed to a cross, but on the third day he will rise from the dead.'"

Then the women remembered Jesus' words. They came back from the tomb and told all these things to the 11 apostles and all the others. Mary Magdalene, Joanna, Mary the mother of James, and the others with them were the ones who told this to the apostles.

But the apostles didn't believe the women, because their words didn't make any sense to them. Luke 24:6-11

So Peter and the other disciple started out for the tomb. Both of them were running, but the other disciple ran faster than Peter and reached the tomb first. He bent over and looked in, and he saw the strips of linen lying there. But he didn't go in. Then Simon Peter came along behind him and went right into the tomb. He also saw the strips of linen lying there, and he saw the funeral cloth that had been wrapped around Jesus' head. The cloth was still lying in its place, separate from the linen. The disciple who'd reached the tomb first then went inside. He saw and believed. Until then they hadn't understood from Scripture that Jesus had to rise from the dead. Then the disciples went back to where they were staying.

But Mary [Magdalene] was still standing outside the tomb, crying. As she cried, she bent over to look into the tomb, and she saw two angels dressed in white. They were seated where Jesus' body had been, one at the head and the other at the feet.

They asked her, "Woman, why are you crying?"

"They've taken my Lord away, and I don't know where they've put him," she answered. Then she turned around and saw Jesus standing there. But she didn't realize that it was Jesus.

He asked her, "Woman, why are you crying? Who are you looking for?"

She thought he was the gardener, so she said, "Sir, if you've carried him away, tell me where you've put him, and I'll go get him."

Jesus said to her, "Mary."

She turned toward him and cried out in the Hebrew language, "*Rabboni!*" (That means Teacher.)

Jesus told her, "Don't hold on to me, because I haven't ascended to the Father yet. Instead, go to those who believe in me and tell them, 'I'm ascending to my Father and your Father, to my God and your God.'"

Mary Magdalene went and told the disciples, "I have seen the Lord!" Then she told them that he'd said these things to her. John 20:3-18

While the women were on their way, some of the guards went into the city and reported everything that had happened to the chief priests. So the chief priests met with the elders and came up with a plan. They gave the soldiers a large amount of money and told them to say, "His disciples came during the night and stole his body while we were sleeping." They added, "If the governor hears this report, we'll make sure you don't get into trouble."

So the soldiers took the money and did as they were told, and their story is still being told among the Jews to this day. Matt. 28:11-15

That same day, two of Jesus' followers were going to a village called Emmaus. It was about seven miles from Jerusalem. They were talking with each other about everything that had happened. As they talked about those things, Jesus himself came up and walked along with them. But they were kept from recognizing him.

Jesus asked them, "What are you talking about as you walk along?"

They stood still and their faces were sad. One of them, named Cleopas, said to Jesus, "Are you the only person visiting Jerusalem who doesn't know about the things that have happened there in the last few days?"

"What things?" Jesus asked.

"About Jesus of Nazareth," they replied. "He was a prophet who was powerful in what he said and did in the sight of God and all the people. The chief priests and our rulers handed him over to be sentenced to death, and they nailed him to a cross, though we had hoped that he was the one who was going to set Israel free. It's now the third day since all that happened, and some of our women have told us an amazing story. Early this morning they went to the tomb, but they didn't find his body there. They came back and told us that they'd seen a vision of angels, who told them Jesus was alive. So some of our friends went to the tomb, and they found that it was empty, just as the women had said. They didn't see Jesus' body there."

Jesus said to them, "How foolish you are! How long it takes you to believe all that the prophets said! Didn't the Messiah have to suffer these things and then receive his glory?"

Jesus explained to them what was said about himself in all the Scriptures, beginning with Moses and all the Prophets.

As they approached the village where they were going, Jesus kept on walking, as if he were going farther. But they tried to convince him not to leave. They said, "Stay with us, because it's nearly evening and the day is almost over." So he went in to stay with them.

When they were together at the table, he took bread, gave thanks, broke it, and began to give it to them. Then their eyes were opened, and they recognized him, and he disappeared from their sight. They said to each other, "Weren't our hearts burning within us as he explained to us what the Scriptures meant as he talked with us on the road?"

They got up and returned at once to Jerusalem. There they found the 11 disciples and those with them all gathered together and saying, "It's true! The Lord has risen! He has appeared to Simon!"

Then the two of them told what had happened to them on the road and how they had recognized Jesus when he broke the bread.

The disciples were still talking about this when Jesus himself suddenly stood among them. He said to them, "Peace be with you!"

They were surprised and frightened because they thought they were seeing a ghost. Jesus said to them, "Why are you so upset? Why do you have doubts in your minds? Look at my hands and my feet. It's me! Touch me and see. A ghost doesn't have a body or bones, but you can see that I do."

After he said that, he showed them his hands and feet. But they still couldn't believe it because they were too delighted and amazed. So Jesus asked them, "Do you have anything here to eat?" They gave him a piece of cooked fish, and he took it and ate it in front of them. Luke 24:13-43

Jesus said again, "May peace be with you! As the Father has sent me, I'm sending you." Then he breathed on them and said, "Receive the Holy Spirit. If you forgive anyone's sins, their sins are forgiven. If you don't forgive them, those sins not forgiven."

Thomas, one of the 12 disciples (he was also called Didymus), wasn't with the others when Jesus came. So they told him, "We've seen the Lord!"

But he said to them, "Unless I see the nail marks in his hands, and put my finger where the nails were, and put my hand into his side where the spear went, I won't believe."

A week later, Jesus' disciples were in the house again. This time Thomas was with them. Even though the doors were locked, Jesus came in and stood among them. He said, "May peace be with you!" Then he said to Thomas, "Put your finger here and look at my hands. Reach out your hand and put it into my side. Stop doubting and believe."

Thomas said to him, "My Lord and my God!"

Then Jesus told him, "Because you've seen me, you have believed. Blessed are those who haven't seen me but have still believed." John 20:21-29

CHAPTER 21

MORE TO COME

Then the 11 disciples went to Galilee, to the mountain where Jesus had told them to go. When they saw him, they worshiped him, though some still had their doubts.

Then Jesus came to them and said, "All authority in heaven and on earth has been given to me. So go and make disciples of all nations. Baptize them in the name of the Father and of the Son and of the Holy Spirit. Teach them to obey everything I have commanded you. And you can be sure that I will always be with you, to the very end of the age." Matt. 28:16-20

He said to them, "Go everywhere in the world and preach the good news to the whole creation. Anyone who believes and is baptized will be saved, but anyone who doesn't believe will be condemned. Those who believe will do miraculous signs. They'll drive out demons in my name, and they'll speak in new tongues. They'll pick up snakes with their hands, and if they drink deadly poison, it won't hurt them at all. When they will place their hands on sick people, the sick will get well." Mark 16:15-18

After this Jesus appeared to his disciples again by the Sea of Tiberias (that is, the Sea of Galilee). Here's what happened. Simon Peter and Thomas were there together with Nathanael from Cana in Galilee, the two sons of Zebedee, and two more disciples.

"I'm going out to fish," Simon Peter told them. They said, "We'll go with you." So they went out and got into the boat, but they didn't catch anything all night.

Early in the morning Jesus stood on the shore, but the disciples didn't realize that it was Jesus.

He called out to them, "Friends, didn't you catch any fish?"

"No!" they answered.

He said, "Throw out your net on the right side of the boat, and you'll find some there." When they did that, they couldn't pull the net back into the boat, because there were so many fish in it.

Then the disciple Jesus loved said to Simon Peter, "It's the Lord!"

As soon as Peter heard that, he put his shirt back on (he'd taken it off to work) and jumped into the water. The other disciples followed in the boat, towing the net full of fish. They weren't far from shore, only about 100 yards away.

When they landed, they saw a fire there with fish on it. There was also some bread. Jesus said to them, "Bring some of the fish you just caught." So Simon Peter climbed back into the boat and dragged the net to shore. It was full of large fish, 153 in all, but even with that many fish in it, the net hadn't torn. Jesus said to them, "Come and have breakfast." None of the disciples dared to ask him, "Who are you?" They knew it was the Lord. Jesus came, took the bread, and gave it to them. He did the same thing with the fish.

This was the third time Jesus had appeared to his disciples after he had been raised from the dead.

When Jesus and the disciples had finished eating, Jesus said to Simon Peter, "Simon, son of John, do you love me more than these others do?"

"Yes, Lord," he answered, "you know that I love you."

Jesus said, "Feed my lambs."

Again, Jesus asked, "Simon, son of John, do you love me?"

He answered, "Yes, Lord, you know that I love you."

Jesus said, "Take care of my sheep."

Jesus said to him a third time, "Simon, son of John, do you love me?"

It made Peter sad that Jesus had asked him a third time, "Do you love me?" He answered, "Lord, you know all things. You know that I love you."

Jesus said, "Feed my sheep. Truly I tell you, when you were younger, you dressed yourself and went wherever you wanted to go. But when you are old, you will stretch out your hands and someone else will dress you and lead you where you don't want to go." Jesus said this to show Peter how he would die and bring glory to God. Then Jesus said to him, "Follow me!"

Peter turned around and saw that the disciple Jesus loved was following them. (He was the one who had leaned back against Jesus at the supper and asked, "Lord, who is going to hand you over to your enemies?") When Peter saw that disciple, he asked, "Lord, what will happen to him?"

Jesus answered, "If I want him to remain alive until I return, what does that matter to you? You must follow me." Because Jesus said this, a rumor spread among the believers that the disciple Jesus loved wouldn't die. But Jesus didn't say he wouldn't die. He only said, "If I want him to remain alive until I return, what does that matter to you?"

This is the disciple [John] who is a witness about these things. He has written them down, and we know that what he says is true. John 21:1-24

Jesus appeared to them over a period of 40 days after his suffering and death, and he proved in many ways that he was alive. During that time, he spoke about the kingdom of God.

One day when Jesus was eating with his apostles, he told them, "Don't leave Jerusalem, but wait for what my Father promised—what you've heard me talk about. John baptized with water, but in a few days, you'll be baptized with the Holy Spirit."

Then the apostles gathered around Jesus and asked him a question. "Lord," they said, "are you now going to give the kingdom back to Israel?"

He answered, "You aren't allowed to know times and dates that the Father has set by his own authority. But you will receive power when the Holy Spirit comes on you. Then you will be my witnesses in Jerusalem, in all Judea and Samaria, and to the farthest point on earth." Acts 1:3-8

Jesus said to them, "This is what I told you while I was still with you. Everything that is written about me in the Law of Moses, the Prophets, and the Psalms must come true."

Then he opened their minds so they could understand the Scriptures. He told them, "This is what is written: The Messiah will suffer and rise from the dead on the third day, and his followers will preach in his name. They will tell others to turn away from their sins and be forgiven. People from every nation will hear about this, beginning in Jerusalem. You have seen these things with your own eyes. I am going to send you what my Father has promised, but for now, stay in the city until you have received power from heaven."

Jesus led his disciples out to the area near Bethany. Then he lifted up his hands and blessed them. While he was blessing them, he left them and was taken up into heaven. Luke 24:44-51

They kept on looking up into the sky while he was going. Suddenly two men dressed in white clothing stood beside them. "Men of Galilee," they asked, "why are you standing here looking at the sky? This same Jesus, who has been taken up from you into heaven, will come back just as you saw him go." Acts 1:10-11

Then they worshiped him and returned to Jerusalem with great joy. Every day they were in the temple, praising God. Luke 24:52-53

Jesus performed many other signs when he was with his disciples. They're not written down in this book. But these signs have been written down so that you may believe that Jesus is the Messiah, the Son of God, and that by believing, you may have life in his name. John 20:30-31

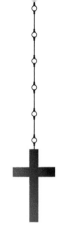

STUDY RESOURCES

REFLECTIONS AND QUESTIONS

Chapter 1 God Reaches Out (p. 1)

Reflect

The story of Jesus does not start at his birth, but at the start of all things. He is described as the Word—the creative power of the universe. He came to us as a human being to bring *life* and *light*.

Angels make two announcements—one to Zechariah and the other to Mary. One is an old man and the other is a young woman. God gave them each a mission.

Both Zechariah and Mary were afraid when they first received their mission. But they both believed that everything is possible for God and said "yes" even though they didn't understand how everything would work out.

Mary hurried to visit Elizabeth, her pregnant relative. Elizabeth called Mary "the mother of my Lord" and rejoiced that she was greatly blessed. Mary praised God for his favor to her and intervention for his people.

Think

* Have you considered that, like Zechariah and Mary, God has a mission planned for you?
* How does this reading affect your thinking about your calling or purpose in life?
* Are you afraid that God will call you to do something for which you don't feel ready? If so, how do the responses of Zechariah and Mary inspire your response?
* What challenges did Mary face? Would you say "yes" to God as Mary did?

Pray

Talk to God in prayer about this reading. In your own words, ask God to show you what it means for your life.

Apply

Look for the phrase in the reading that most catches your attention. Underline or highlight it. Reflect on how it applies to you.

Act

What concrete action will you take to apply your prayer and reflection in your daily life?

Discuss

1. The story of Jesus begins with words and phrases such as life, light, children of God, glory, and grace. Which word or phrase stands out the most to you? What do you find interesting about it?
2. If you were Mary, what would you be feeling and thinking about your pregnancy? How might others react to your situation?
3. Zechariah foretold that his son, John, would prepare the way for the Lord by telling people how they could find salvation. What might lead someone to feel that they need to be saved from something?

_____

_____

_____

_____

_____

_____

_____

_____

Chapter 2 A Special Birth (p. 7)

Reflect

Joseph received warnings in two dreams: first to accept Jesus and his mother Mary, and then to save them from death by fleeing to Egypt. His purpose in life was to watch over Jesus. Joseph believed, and he acted on faith. His decision could not have been easy, but he followed God's direction for his life.

Notice in this reading all the people who seek Jesus to worship him—the shepherds, Simeon, Anna, and the wise men from the East. Each one was called in a different way to seek the Lord, because every person has a different story.

Later we find Jesus in the temple speaking to the Jewish teachers. From a young age, Jesus understood his calling to do the will of God his Father.

Think

- Are you able to listen to God and his messengers? How can you become more open to God in your life?
- Accepting a calling from God may involve leaving your comfort zone. Are you willing to do this?
- How would you feel if you were the shepherds or wise men visiting the baby Jesus?
- The people in this reading publicly acknowledged Jesus. Is there anything that stops you from doing this?

Pray

Talk to God in prayer about this reading. In your own words, ask God to show you what it means for your life.

Apply

Look for the phrase in the reading that most catches your attention. Underline or highlight it. Reflect on how it applies to you.

Act

What concrete action will you take to apply your prayer and reflection in your daily life?

Discuss

1. Jesus' birth was quite different from what might be expected for the Savior of the world. Instead of being surrounded by royal attendants and rituals, he was surrounded by animals, along with their sounds and smells. What do the circumstances of Jesus' birth say about God?

2. Joseph and Mary were in a situation that likely felt both wonderful and terrifying. When have you experienced a situation that felt both wonderful and terrifying? What fears or hopes crossed your mind?

3. Isaiah prophesied that a virgin would miraculously have a baby who would be known as Immanuel, which means "God with us." Have you ever felt that God was with you? In what area of your life would you like to have God's presence?

_____

_____

_____

_____

_____

_____

_____

_____

_____

_____

Chapter 3 Preparing the Way *(p. 13)*

Reflect

John the Baptist had decided to dedicate his life to prayer and living in the desert. That's where the Word of God called him to proclaim a message of repentance and announce the good news of Jesus. His mission involved years of prayer and listening to discern the will of God.

Jesus stood in line with sinners waiting to be baptized by John. It is unclear why he did that, but the voice of the Father confirmed that Jesus is his beloved Son who does what is right.

Jesus prepared himself for his public mission by going into the desert where he was tempted. Satan tried to tempt him by using Scripture, obviously taken out of context. Jesus responded with Scripture.

John proclaimed Jesus is the Lamb of God who takes away the sin of the world. He is the one to follow.

Think

- To understand your purpose in life, how much time do you devote to listening to God?
- What steps do you take to set aside a special time regularly for prayer?
- In your life, how might you share the good news about Jesus or speak up about injustice?
- What are the temptations stopping you from carrying out your calling from God?

Pray

Talk to God in prayer about this reading. In your own words, ask God to show you what it means for your life.

Apply

Look for the phrase in the reading that most catches your attention. Underline or highlight it. Reflect on how it applies to you.

Act

What concrete action will you take to apply your prayer and reflection in your daily life?

Discuss

1. As John baptized people, he gave some especially harsh warnings to the religious leaders of the day. What was he trying to say to them, and why do you think he was so hard on them?
2. When Jesus was baptized by John, a voice spoke from heaven saying, "You are my beloved Son. I'm very pleased with you." There was nothing Jesus did to earn his heavenly Father's love; the Father loved him no matter what. When have you sensed unconditional love from God or from someone else?
3. When have you experienced temptations that are tough to resist? How can Jesus' response during his time in the desert guide you when you feel tested?

Chapter 4 Jesus Starts His Mission (p. 17)

Reflect

Jesus started his mission by calling the followers he wanted. His first disciples left everything to follow him.

Jesus participated in the daily life of his people—he blessed a wedding with wonderful wine.

With Nicodemus, Jesus spoke of a new spiritual birth. He explained that it means we must believe in the Son who was sent by God. We begin to follow Jesus by believing in him and his promise of eternal life.

Jesus had no problem talking to a woman who was an outcast Samaritan and asking her to trust that he is the "living water." He knows about our human life with its mistakes and sins. He accepted the woman and spoke to her about eternal life.

Jesus announced that the official's son would be healed. The official took Jesus at his word—and it happened at that very time! Jesus gives signs to those who seek to believe.

Think

- Can you say you are a follower—a true disciple—of Jesus?
- If you were to come to Jesus like Nicodemus, what do you think he would ask of you?
- When do you raise objections to Jesus' teaching, like the Samaritan woman?
- Where do you look for signs to believe that Jesus is calling you?

Pray

Talk to God in prayer about this reading. In your own words, ask God to show you what it means for your life.

Apply

Look for the phrase in the reading that most catches your attention. Underline or highlight it. Reflect on how it applies to you.

Act

What concrete action will you take to apply your prayer and reflection in your daily life?

Discuss

1. This chapter includes one of the best-known passages in the Bible—John 3:16—which declares, "God loved the world so much that he gave his one and only Son so that anyone who believes in him may not die but have eternal life." Why do you think this verse has been so meaningful to so many people who follow Jesus?
2. Jews and Samaritans were hostile toward each other, and women were not respected in either culture. Jesus crossed major boundaries by sharing his message of hope with a Samaritan woman. What cultural and ethnic boundaries do you see today, and how might Jesus try to cross them? How might you cross them?
3. When Jesus continued to talk with the Samaritan woman, he could see the parts of her life of which she had been ashamed and had tried to hide from other people. How do you think Jesus would respond to the parts of your life that you try to hide from others?

Chapter 5 Opposition Begins *(p. 25)*

Reflect

The Scripture passage that Jesus read is from the Old Testament book of Isaiah. He spoke about the prophecy and explained it was being fulfilled. Although many people admired Jesus, other people in his hometown didn't want to accept his message.

Peter's encounter with Jesus was life-changing. Seeing the miraculous catch of fish, and recognizing himself as a sinner, Peter asked Jesus to leave him alone. But instead, Jesus entrusted him with a mission.

Jesus went in search of the most despised people in his culture— public sinners and tax collectors who served the foreign oppressors. Unlike the religious leaders, he looked at them with compassion and chose them.

Jesus healed people on the Sabbath— the sacred day of rest— when the Law did not permit it. Jesus's authority goes beyond the old religious laws, and that is why he is Lord of the Sabbath.

Think

- Simon Peter asked Jesus to leave because he was afraid he was not fit for Jesus. Do you also feel that you are unworthy of Jesus? Do you realize that Jesus loves just you as you are?
- Is there a situation in your life where Jesus wants you to rise up to follow him, like the man he healed who was unable to walk? Make a list of the things that keep you down.
- Matthew was ashamed of his life as a tax collector for the Romans. He was unworthy in the eyes of the people, yet Jesus called him to be a disciple. Can you accept that Jesus looks upon you with mercy and chooses you?
- Jesus came to proclaim the good news. Do you welcome him and his teachings, or is your belief system bound by other people's rules and opinions?

Pray

Talk to God in prayer about this reading. In your own words, ask God to show you what it means for your life.

Apply

Look for the phrase in the reading that most catches your attention. Underline or highlight it. Reflect on how it applies to you.

Act

What concrete action will you take to apply your prayer and reflection in your daily life?

Discuss

1. Imagine being in the synagogue and seeing Jesus as he reads Isaiah 61, proclaiming that God has chosen him to fulfill the prophecy and announce the good news. How do you think you would have felt? How would you have described what happened to friends who weren't there?

2. When some people tore apart a roof and lowered their disabled friend down in front of Jesus, he said two surprising things: "Friend, your sins are forgiven" and "get up, take your mat, and go home." Why do you think Jesus made statements about both spiritual healing and physical healing? What does it tell us about Jesus?

3. Jesus praised the friends of the disabled man for their great faith. Do you know someone who has great faith? What do you find appealing about their life and choices?

_____

_____

_____

_____

_____

Chapter 6 Teaching the People (p. 35)

Reflect

The evil spirits acknowledged Jesus' authority by telling him, "You are the Son of God." Jesus had the authority to choose his 12 disciples.

Jesus, in his sermon on the mountain, gave us guidelines for life and happiness. He taught that his disciples must be *salt* to preserve the world from corruption, and they must be *light* to illuminate it. That will be our testimony for the world to believe—a new way of life that brings the fulfillment of God's law.

The topics in Jesus' sermon are vital, such as our love for everyone—even our enemies, our prayers to the Father, and the relationship Jesus' disciples should have with the things of this world.

His teaching produces a vital change that will be seen in our lives. If we claim Jesus as Lord, we must do what he says. Listening to and obeying Jesus is like building a house on a solid foundation.

Think

- Is Jesus calling you to be his disciple? What are you doing to recognize his call and respond?
- How do you compare the ways in which Jesus says people are blessed to the world's way of thinking? What are the blessings in your life?
- In the Lord's prayer, we ask God to forgive us as we forgive others. How can you move from just knowing about forgiveness to forgiving others—or asking them to forgive you?
- What are things you can do to put Jesus' teaching into practice?

Pray

Talk to God in prayer about this reading. In your own words, ask God to show you what it means for your life.

Apply

Look for the phrase in the reading that most catches your attention. Underline or highlight it. Reflect on how it applies to you.

Act

What concrete action will you take to apply your prayer and reflection in your daily life?

Discuss

1. When Jesus taught the crowd on a mountainside, he made amazing, but counterintuitive, promises about the people who will be blessed. If you had been among the crowd and heard all of Jesus' promises about being blessed, which would stand out the most to you and why?

2. Perhaps Jesus' most radical teaching is that we are to love our enemies and pray for those who hurt us. Why would Jesus want us to do this? As you think about your own enemies, or those who have hurt you, how could you take a step toward following Jesus' teaching?

3. In the midst of our anxiety and concerns, Jesus tells us not to worry because God will take care of our needs, and that it's more important to focus on putting God's kingdom first. What is causing you anxiety right now? Are you able to trust God to help you with that?

Chapter 7 Accused of Using Evil Powers (p. 45)

Reflect

A Roman officer acknowledged Jesus' authority. He said to Jesus, "Just say the word," because the word of Jesus has power.

Jesus came across a funeral procession for a young man and called the young man back from death to life again.

Jesus did not seek wise or powerful people, nor the religious leaders. Knowledgeable and sophisticated people were more concerned with their own arguments than with knowing Jesus.

The religious leaders' envy of Jesus' power is obvious, and they claimed his power was evil. But Jesus delivers people from evil with the power of good.

Jesus taught that people who listen to God and do what God wants are his family.

Jesus spoke in stories to make his message understandable. He sowed a message that will change people's lives, but the evil one sows sin in people's lives.

Think

- Are you convinced that the word of Jesus has power? How does it reveal itself to you?
- It did not matter to Jesus that the young man was already dead; Jesus called him back to life. At what times have you felt "dead" in some way? Do you think Jesus can raise you out of that situation?
- Jesus reveals himself to people who are humble. Are you willing to come to him with humility, so he will reveal himself to you?
- Jesus told a story of a man who planted good seed in his field, but then an enemy came and planted weeds. Both are sown in your life—can you identify them?

Pray

Talk to God in prayer about this reading. In your own words, ask God to show you what it means for your life.

Apply

Look for the phrase in the reading that most catches your attention. Underline or highlight it. Reflect on how it applies to you.

Act

What concrete action will you take to apply your prayer and reflection in your daily life?

Discuss

1. Jesus praised the Roman officer's faith. What was it about the officer's description of authority that shows his great faith? In what ways would you like your own faith to be like the Roman officer's?

2. When Jesus heard that his mother and brothers were standing outside, he said, "Anyone who does what my heavenly Father wants is my brother and sister and mother." Who do you consider your family, and what determines that? How does Jesus' definition of family challenge or expand your definition?

3. Jesus told a story of a farmer who sowed seed in four different places: on the road, in rocky soil, in thorny soil, and in good soil. If the seed is God's message, which of these four soils best describes you? Why do you think God is so generous to sow seed in all kinds of soil?

_____

_____

_____

_____

_____

_____

_____

Chapter 8 Calming a Storm (p. 55)

Reflect

In the middle of the storm Jesus asked his disciples, "Where is your faith?" He called them to have courage and trust him.

Once again, it was the evil spirits that recognized Jesus is the "Son of the Most High God." The person who was possessed was called to announce the wonders of God.

The woman who was sick sought just to touch the cloak of Jesus. She had great faith she would be healed.

Jesus went to the synagogue leader's house whose daughter died. But death is not an obstacle for Jesus. He is the creator of life and called her to get up.

Jesus stated that the harvest is large, but there are few workers to gather it. This statement is about his kingdom and the people who share his message. They go like sheep amongst wolves—consider that John the Baptist was beheaded.

Think

- Jesus asks you in the midst of your storms, "Where is your faith?" How do you respond?
- No matter how bad things are going, Jesus will work miracles in your life. Are you ready to accept him and tell people how much he has done for you?
- The suffering woman reached out with courage and great faith just to touch Jesus' cloak. When have you been able to reach out in faith to Jesus?
- Jesus calls you to go like a sheep in the midst of wolves. What might that look like in your life? Are you willing to be one of his workers?

Pray

Talk to God in prayer about this reading. In your own words, ask God to show you what it means for your life.

Apply

Look for the phrase in the reading that most catches your attention. Underline or highlight it. Reflect on how it applies to you.

Act

What concrete action will you take to apply your prayer and reflection in your daily life?

Discuss

1. Jesus calmed a raging storm by ordering the wind to stop and the waves to be calm. How are Jesus' words relevant to the storms you face in your emotions, circumstances, and relationships?
2. Before Jesus sent out his 12 disciples to announce God's kingdom and heal the sick, he described the harvest as great but the workers as few. Would you say that this remains true today, or not? What makes you think that?
3. Jesus warned that, "Whoever doesn't pick up their cross and follow me is not worthy of me. Whoever finds their life will lose it, but whoever loses their life because of me will find it." What do you think you would find if you followed Jesus? What do you think you might lose? Is the trade-off worth it? Why or why not?

Chapter 9 Feeding the Hungry Crowds (p. 63)

Reflect

Jesus instructed his disciples to feed the large crowd but did not send them to buy food. He knew he would provide it. After this miracle, Jesus went off by himself to pray.

The disciples were in a boat at night being tossed about by the waves. They were terrified when they saw Jesus walking on the water. But he told them not to be afraid—an encouragement that is repeated many times in the Bible.

Jesus called Peter to come to him. Peter bravely stepped onto the water but started to sink when he took his attention off Jesus. Jesus asked him, "You have such little faith! Why did you doubt?"

Jesus taught that he is the Bread of Life which came down from heaven. Whoever feeds on him will have eternal life. His teaching was very difficult for some people, so they stopped following him. Jesus asked his disciples if they also wanted to leave. Peter replied, "Lord, where would we go to? You have the words of eternal life."

Think

- In what way is feeding the hungry a part of your calling and mission as a Christian?
- How is Jesus perhaps inviting you to leave a place of safety and step out in faith toward him?
- In the midst of turmoil, are you able to hear the Lord telling you, "Don't be afraid"? How can you find the courage to trust him?
- Do you believe Jesus has the words of eternal life? How does that help you to follow him?

Pray

Talk to God in prayer about this reading. In your own words, ask God to show you what it means for your life.

Apply

Look for the phrase in the reading that most catches your attention. Underline or highlight it. Reflect on how it applies to you.

Act

What concrete action will you take to apply your prayer and reflection in your daily life?

Discuss

1. On two different occasions, Jesus took a few loaves of bread and fed thousands of people. What motivated Jesus to do this? What does this say about Jesus' care for people's needs? How does he care for you?

2. When Jesus beckoned Peter to come to him on the water, what do you admire about Peter's actions and attitudes? What did he do that caused him not to succeed?

3. Jesus warned that, just as a tiny amount of yeast can affect a large amount of dough, the false teaching of the Pharisees and Sadducees could contaminate much around them. What do you think Jesus found so appalling about the actions and attitudes of these religious leaders?

Chapter 10 Seen in God's Glory (p. *73)*

Reflect

Jesus asked: "Who do people say I am?" Simon Peter replied, "You are the Messiah, the Son of the living God." Although Peter recognized the Messiah, he tried to prevent Jesus from going to Jerusalem to be killed. "Get behind me, Satan!" was Jesus' firm response.

The most challenging calling for disciples of Jesus is to be prepared to deny themselves and commit to follow him at whatever cost.

Jesus was revealed on the mountain as a divine person. The Father confirmed that, "This is my beloved Son, and I'm very pleased with him. Listen to him!"

Jesus welcomed little children. He said, "Whoever becomes humble like this little child is the greatest in the kingdom of heaven."

Our witness about Jesus's love should be first and foremost shown through love and forgiveness of others.

Think

- Even when we acknowledge Jesus as Lord, we can obstruct his plan for the salvation of all people. Does your behavior prevent Jesus from revealing himself to others?
- We are called to let go of everything that prevents us from being a true disciple of Jesus —such as pride, selfishness, greed, or fear. How do you feel about making that level of commitment?
- Do you listen—that is, obey and follow Jesus—as the Father has asked you to do?
- What does it mean for you to humble yourself and become like a child?

Pray

Talk to God in prayer about this reading. In your own words, ask God to show you what it means for your life.

Apply

Look for the phrase in the reading that most catches your attention. Underline or highlight it. Reflect on how it applies to you.

Act

What concrete action will you take to apply your prayer and reflection in your daily life?

Discuss

1. Jesus asked his disciples two key questions: "Who do people say I am?" and "Who do you say I am?" If a survey about Jesus was taken today, who do you think people would say he is? How would you answer?

2. The father of a boy controlled by an evil spirit cried out, "I do believe! Help me overcome my unbelief!" He let Jesus know that he did believe in him, and yet there were parts of his faith that needed help. In what ways is your faith in Jesus already strong? Where does it need help?

3. The culture of Jesus' time didn't always treasure children. Yet Jesus told his disciples that they need to welcome children and become like them. What is it about children that Jesus found so important?

_____

_____

_____

_____

_____

_____

_____

Chapter 11 Claiming God's Name (p. 81)

Reflect

People made excuses not to follow Jesus. His challenging response was that anyone who starts to follow but then looks back isn't fit for service in God's kingdom.

Jesus promised, "If anyone believes in me, rivers of living water will flow from inside them." He was referring to the Holy Spirit.

Jesus came to save, not to condemn. We see this clearly with the woman who was caught committing adultery. He said to her accusers, "If any of you has never sinned, he can be the first to throw a stone at her."

Jesus stated that he is not from this world but came from above. He called himself "I Am"—the Hebrew sacred name of God. The religious leaders were so angry they tried to stone him.

Think

- What are the excuses or obstacles that stop you from following Jesus?
- Jesus obeyed the will of the Father. How willing are you to obey God even if doing so might cause you problems?
- Are you quick to condemn other people who do wrong? What can you do to follow Jesus' example to show mercy?
- We are called to spread the light of Jesus in the darkness around us. How might you live in the light?

Pray

Talk to God in prayer about this reading. In your own words, ask God to show you what it means for your life.

Apply

Look for the phrase in the reading that most catches your attention. Underline or highlight it. Reflect on how it applies to you.

Act

What concrete action will you take to apply your prayer and reflection in your daily life?

Discuss

1. The religious leaders used a woman caught in adultery to trap Jesus in a position where he had to choose between law and grace. How does his response turn the tables on this trap—for both the leaders and the woman?
2. Jesus explained to the Jews that his truth will set them free. What do you think they needed freedom from? In what areas of your life would you like freedom? What might that look like?
3. Jesus described the devil as the father of lies who leads people to believe they are less than what God has intended for them. What types of lies do you believe about yourself and our world? What truth can you keep in mind to respond to those lies in the future?

Chapter 12 Who Is He? *(p. 89)*

Reflect

Jesus was asked about what we must do to receive eternal life. His answer ended with an example of what it means to love others. We will be judged by how we treat other people.

Martha was disturbed that her sister Mary didn't help her to attend to their guests. Jesus reminded her, and us, that it is important to take the time to listen to him.

Jesus healed the man who had been born blind. When the blind man witnessed to the Pharisees about Jesus and his power to heal, they became angry and threw him out of the synagogue.

Jesus is the Good Shepherd who takes care of us, his sheep. He leads us to the sheep pen, meaning heaven.

The people asked Jesus for the truth about who he is. He replied, "I and the Father are one." Once again, the religious leaders tried to stone him because he claimed to be God.

Think

- Do you worry about death? If so, what should you do about it?
- What does it mean for you to love your neighbor as you love yourself?
- In what ways are you blind to the truth of who Jesus is?
- Jesus said his sheep would know him and follow his voice. Do you see yourself as one of the sheep cared for by the Good Shepherd?

Pray

Talk to God in prayer about this reading. In your own words, ask God to show you what it means for your life.

Apply

Look for the phrase in the reading that most catches your attention. Underline or highlight it. Reflect on how it applies to you.

Act

What concrete action will you take to apply your prayer and reflection in your daily life?

Discuss

1. When an authority on the law asked Jesus, "Who is my neighbor," Jesus told the story of a severely beaten man who was rescued by a Samaritan. Keeping in mind the huge ethnic, cultural, and religious division between first-century Jews and Samaritans, how would Jesus want you to act toward people with whom you disagree or disrespect?

2. When Jesus visited his friends Mary and Martha, what was it about Mary's choice that made it better than Martha's? How can you similarly make a better choice in the future?

3. Jesus said that he came that we may have life in the fullest possible way. Based on what you have read or know about Jesus, what would make the life Jesus offers better than other lifestyles?

_____

_____

_____

_____

_____

_____

_____

_____

_____

_____

Chapter 13 Raising the Dead (p. 97)

Reflect

Jesus told a story about a banquet where many of the invited guests made excuses. Jesus's invitation to God's kingdom is open to everyone. However, to enter we must accept his invitation.

The stories of the lost sheep and the lost coin illustrate that God cares for each of us as individuals. Jesus told another story of the son who wasted his inheritance. His father was waiting for him and lovingly received him back. In contrast, the other son resented the father showing mercy.

In the story of the poor man and the rich man who both died, no one could cross the chasm between them. It offers a new perspective on what happened with Lazarus, the friend of Jesus who had been dead for several days when Jesus arrived. Jesus is the resurrection and the life. He thanked God for hearing him, then called Lazarus to come out of the tomb.

Think

- Jesus extends to us an invitation to his kingdom. What excuses have you used to reject his invitation to participate?
- If you compare the story of the merciful father to your life, how do you experience God's unconditional love?
- Mary complained because Jesus was not there when her brother died after she had called for him to come. How do you respond when God doesn't do what you ask him to do, or asks you to wait?
- Jesus has the power to resurrect the dead. If you are in a very difficult situation, do you believe that Jesus has the power to call you out of it?

Pray

Talk to God in prayer about this reading. In your own words, ask God to show you what it means for your life.

Apply

Look for the phrase in the reading that most catches your attention. Underline or highlight it. Reflect on how it applies to you.

Act

What concrete action will you take to apply your prayer and reflection in your daily life?

Discuss

1. Jesus shared a story about a shepherd who left his sheep to find the one sheep that was lost. How does it feel to hear that Jesus will do the same to find you when you are lost?

2. Jesus painted a vivid contrast between the attitude of the younger son who received a warm welcome from his father that he felt he didn't deserve, and the older son who felt unappreciated for his years of faithful service. When do you feel more like the younger son? When do you feel more like the older son?

3. Jesus warned his disciples and the Pharisees: "You can't serve God and money at the same time." Jesus was referring to people's tendency to be more devoted to money, and all money can buy, than to him. How is money a temptation for you? What or who tends to be your master?

_____

_____

_____

_____

_____

_____

_____

_____

Chapter 14 Welcomed as King *(p. 109)*

Reflect

Prayer is important to Jesus. He explained it with the stories of the widow who persisted in petitioning the judge, and of the tax collector whose prayer was heard because of his humility.

A man claimed that he had kept the Jewish law since childhood. Jesus invited him to take another step—to let go of his riches and follow him, but the man didn't want to follow Jesus that much.

Jesus announced to his disciples that they were going to Jerusalem—where the religious leaders will sentence him to death, but three days later he will rise from the dead.

James and his brother John requested privileged positions in the Kingdom of God. Jesus retorted that they should be willing to be a slave to all the others.

When Zacchaeus, the chief tax collector, met Jesus he demonstrated his change of heart by giving away half of his possessions and returning four times more than he stole.

Think

- The Lord instructs us to pray always without getting discouraged. How is your prayer life, and what can you do to make it more inspiring?
- The rich man went away sad because he was not ready to give up wealth to follow Jesus. Do you worry about things Jesus might ask you to give up? How does letting go of things bring you peace?
- What does it mean for you to put others first and serve them?
- Jesus assured Zacchaeus that salvation had come to his house. Has salvation come into your life? What is your attitude toward Jesus?

Pray

Talk to God in prayer about this reading. In your own words, ask God to show you what it means for your life.

Apply

Look for the phrase in the reading that most catches your attention. Underline or highlight it. Reflect on how it applies to you.

Act

What concrete action will you take to apply your prayer and reflection in your daily life?

Discuss

1. Jesus healed ten men but only one returned to thank him. What is the difference between the attitude of that man and of the other nine? Where do you see traces of your own attitude in the one man? Or in the other nine?

2. How was the Pharisee's attitude different from the tax collector's? In what ways might the attitudes of the Pharisee and the tax collector compare with the attitudes of the workers who all got paid the same wage no matter how long they worked?

3. When Jesus entered Jerusalem on a donkey (now celebrated on Palm Sunday), the crowd spread cloaks and palm branches on the road ahead of Jesus (a traditional royal welcome). The people shouted, "Hosanna" (a Hebrew word meaning "save us") as Jesus entered Jerusalem. What do you think the people wanted Jesus to save them from? What can Jesus save people from today?

Chapter 15 Authority Questioned *(p. 119)*

Reflect

The temple in Jerusalem was a sacred place, but money changers and merchants in the temple exploited it for themselves. Jesus threw them out.

Visitors from Greece wanted to see Jesus. He taught them that he must die to be glorified and draw all people to himself. He is the light for us to follow as children of light to overcome darkness in this world.

The religious rulers demanded to know who gave Jesus the authority to teach the people. Jesus stated that his authority came from the Father who told him what to say.

In the story of the father with two sons, one finally obeys his father, but the other only says he will obey. A person who hears the words of Jesus but doesn't act on them doesn't truly accept his message.

In the story of the vineyard, the tenants murdered the owner's servants and his son. Similarly, God had sent prophets, like John the Baptist, but they had been killed and the religious rulers later crucified Jesus.

Jesus denounced the religious leaders for their conceit, false teaching, and hypocrisy.

Think

- How might Jesus react toward you if you abuse religion to make money or gain status?
- What does it mean for you to follow the light of Jesus' teachings and example?
- Do you accept the authority of Jesus as the Lord in your life? What can you do to obey him more fully?
- Which of the two sons in the story most describes you?

Pray

Talk to God in prayer about this reading. In your own words, ask God to show you what it means for your life.

Apply

Look for the phrase in the reading that most catches your attention. Underline or highlight it. Reflect on how it applies to you.

Act

What concrete action will you take to apply your prayer and reflection in your daily life?

Discuss

1. Why would the tax collectors for the Roman occupiers, and prostitutes, be quicker to respond to Jesus than the religious rulers? What could that mean for you and the people you know?

2. Jesus avoided the religious leaders' trap by teaching that the emperor Caesar had a rightful claim on their lives, as does God. But Jesus' own life showed that obedience to God is more important than anything else. Do you feel any tension between obeying both your government and God? If so, what do you think Jesus wants you to do?

3. Jesus proclaimed that the two most important commandments are to love God totally and to love your neighbors. Why are these two the most important? What would it look like for you to love God with all your heart, soul, and mind? How would that help you to love other people?

Chapter 16 Talking About the Future *(p. 129)*

Reflect

Jesus predicted that wars and disasters would come, and his followers would be persecuted. But he promised his message of love, hope, and salvation will always be with us.

Jesus warned us not to be preoccupied with the distractions and worries of this life. We do not know when we will be called to meet God and face judgment. We must be prepared.

Jesus cares for people. He taught that we serve him by serving the least important people. If we truly follow Jesus, we must follow his example.

Jesus showed love and mercy to the woman who showed devotion to him. He told a story about the importance of forgiveness. God forgives us so much.

Think

- Many people are afraid of the end of the world. What would you say to these people based on the message of Jesus?
- Jesus assured us he will return. How can you be prepared? How can you help others to be prepared also?
- Jesus described the things God the Father will ask us in the final judgment. When do you, or can you, help people most in need?
- Jesus promises to forgive you if you repent of your sins. Are you willing to ask for his forgiveness? How is your repentance demonstrated in your daily life?

Pray

Talk to God in prayer about this reading. In your own words, ask God to show you what it means for your life.

Apply

Look for the phrase in the reading that most catches your attention. Underline or highlight it. Reflect on how it applies to you.

Act

What concrete action will you take to apply your prayer and reflection in your daily life?

Discuss

1. Why did Jesus praise the poor woman who gave two small copper coins? How would you have felt if you were one of the wealthy people standing nearby?
2. What do you think Jesus meant when he taught that if someone has been given a lot, a lot more will be expected of him. What have you been given? Are you taking care of what you've been given as much as God wants?
3. Jesus praises those who take care of the most vulnerable people because it's like taking care of him. Who are the most vulnerable people around you? What would it look like to take care of them as if they were Jesus himself?

Chapter 17 Betrayed by a Friend *(p. 137)*

Reflect

Even Jesus, who was so loving, had friends who betrayed or abandoned him. Judas betrayed Jesus with a kiss for money. When Jesus asked his closest disciples to pray for him in his distress, they fell asleep. All of Jesus' friends ran away when he was arrested.

As an example of humility, Jesus washed the feet of his disciples during their final meal together, which was a servant's job.

Jesus taught about the importance of love. He was willing to sacrifice his life for us. We will want to obey his teaching if we love him. Just as he loves us, he commanded his followers to love one another.

Jesus promised his disciples the Father would send the Holy Spirit, who would stay with them forever and remind them of everything Jesus had said. The Holy Spirit is our helper and counsellor when we accept Jesus.

Think

- You may also have been betrayed or abandoned by a person close to you. What is your reaction to the betrayal of Jesus?
- Jesus asks you to give yourself to the humble service of other people. Through what service do you demonstrate that you follow Jesus?
- What does it mean to you that Jesus is the way, the truth, and the life to reach God the Father?
- Do you ask for help and guidance from the Holy Spirit? How does God speak to you?

Pray

Talk to God in prayer about this reading. In your own words, ask God to show you what it means for your life.

Apply

Look for the phrase in the reading that most catches your attention. Underline or highlight it. Reflect on how it applies to you.

Act

What concrete action will you take to apply your prayer and reflection in your daily life?

Discuss

1. As the disciples' usual means of travel was walking, their feet would have been dirty most of the time. What was Jesus communicating when he insisted on washing their feet? How could we follow Jesus' example today?

2. Jesus taught his followers, "If you do love one another, then everyone will know that you are my disciples." What messages do Jesus' followers communicate today by the ways they love—or don't love—each other?

3. Peter pulled out a sword and sliced off the ear of the high priest's slave when Jesus was arrested. But Jesus healed the man's ear. What does that say about how Jesus views people who oppose him? What would it look like to follow Jesus' example when you feel that you want to retaliate against those who have wronged you?

Chapter 18 Facing False Charges *(p. 151)*

Reflect

The religious and political leaders gathered to conspire against Jesus. They brought in false witnesses who couldn't agree about the accusations. But he was beaten and sentenced to death anyway.

Peter was afraid and denied Jesus. He wept when he heard the rooster crow and remembered Jesus had said he would deny him.

Judas was ashamed and tried to return the money he received for betraying Jesus. Then he committed suicide.

The Jewish leaders were not permitted to crucify anyone. They resorted to lying to Pilate, the Roman governor, to get him to condemn Jesus. Pilate tried to release Jesus, but the Jewish leaders claimed Jesus was a threat to Roman rule.

Even the crowd was deceived. The people who had welcomed Jesus as a king just a week before, now shouted for him to be crucified.

Think

- Have you faced false accusations? What do you learn from Jesus' trial about how to respond when it happens to you?
- Jesus was mocked and abused. There are many forms of abuse today. What do you do when you see others being abused? Do you stay quiet, or do you get involved to support them?
- Have you been tempted to deny that you are a Christian to avoid trouble or blend in better?
- Sometimes our society chooses to do what is wrong. How do you show that you believe in doing what is right?

Pray

Talk to God in prayer about this reading. In your own words, ask God to show you what it means for your life.

Apply

Look for the phrase in the reading that most catches your attention. Underline or highlight it. Reflect on how it applies to you.

Act

What concrete action will you take to apply your prayer and reflection in your daily life?

Discuss

1. Peter, who had been one of Jesus' closest followers, denied knowing Jesus three times. Upon realizing what he had done, Peter broke down and wept. If you encountered Peter as he was crying, what do you think he would say? What would you say to him?
2. As Pilate tried to decide what to do with Jesus, he asked, "What is truth?" What was the truth about Jesus that Pilate didn't understand? How does that truth speak to your life today?
3. Pilate took a long time before deciding what to do with Jesus and seemed very conflicted about whether to give in to the crowd's wishes to crucify Jesus. What motivated Pilate to kill Jesus? Why do you think he was hesitant? What would you have done if you were in Pilate's situation?

Chapter 19 Nailed to a Cross (p. 157)

Reflect

After the Roman soldiers whipped Jesus, they made fun of him. Then they forced him to carry his own cross to the place of execution until he couldn't carry it any longer.

The Scriptures of the Old Testament are fulfilled by Jesus. He is the Messiah, and he suffered this awful death to save humankind.

As Jesus was being nailed to a cross, he said, "Father, forgive them, because they don't know what they're doing." Then he spoke words of encouragement to the other people.

Not only did Jesus experience the agony of hanging on the cross, but he also suffered the pain of being abandoned by his Father for the first time.

After Jesus died, two of his disciples, who had followed Jesus in secret, came to take his body. The religious leaders were concerned the body would be stolen, so Pilate sealed and guarded the tomb.

Think

- Jesus forgave his executioners. How does that make you feel about the forgiveness Jesus offers you? How do you treat people who mistreat you?
- The soldiers took Jesus' clothes. What do you do when you see powerful people taking from people who are vulnerable? Are you willing to object?
- Like Jesus, when have you felt God has abandoned you? If so, can you express that in prayer and listen to what God wants to tell you?
- At what times have you been a secret follower of Jesus?

Pray

Talk to God in prayer about this reading. In your own words, ask God to show you what it means for your life.

Apply

Look for the phrase in the reading that most catches your attention. Underline or highlight it. Reflect on how it applies to you.

Act

What concrete action will you take to apply your prayer and reflection in your daily life?

Discuss

1. Why did Jesus have to die on the cross? John the Baptist called Jesus "the Lamb of God." How does Jesus' death connect to the lambs the priests sacrificed in the temple for the people's sins?
2. One of the criminals being crucified alongside Jesus joined in mocking Jesus, while the other criminal asked Jesus to remember him when Jesus came to his kingdom. Jesus replied to the second man, "Truly I tell you, today you will be with me in Paradise." What could Jesus mean by this?
3. When the Roman commander saw how Jesus died, he proclaimed, "He had to be the Son of God!" What aspect of Jesus' death do you think led him to that conclusion? What would it take for you to agree with the Roman commander that Jesus is the Son of God?

_____

_____

_____

_____

_____

_____

_____

_____

Chapter 20 Back from the Dead (p. 163)

Reflect

Jesus' disciples were devastated because of his crucifixion and death. They went to the grave expecting to find a dead body, but he was not there. Jesus appeared first to Mary Magdalene, who shared the good news with the disciples.

The chief priests bribed the Roman guards to report that the disciples stole the body while the guards were all asleep.

Many of Jesus' followers scattered because they feared what might happen to them. Jesus encountered two on the road to Emmaus, but they did not recognize him at first. They said it felt like their hearts were burning when Jesus explained the Scriptures to them.

Jesus suddenly appeared to some of his disciples and ate a piece of fish to show he was alive. He breathed the Holy Spirit on the disciples and instructed them to continue his mission.

Thomas didn't believe Jesus was back from the dead until he saw him. Jesus said, "Blessed are those who haven't seen me but still believe."

Think

- Do you really believe the witnesses of the resurrection? If so, what causes you to believe? If not, what hinders this belief?
- In what ways has encountering the risen Jesus become real to you?
- What will take for you to be transformed from being a follower of Jesus to a disciple spreading his message?
- Do you need to see in order to believe? Imagine Jesus offering to you his wounds to touch and see.

Pray

Talk to God in prayer about this reading. In your own words, ask God to show you what it means for your life.

Apply

Look for the phrase in the reading that most catches your attention. Underline or highlight it. Reflect on how it applies to you.

Act

What concrete action will you take to apply your prayer and reflection in your daily life?

Discuss

1. Why would the chief priests bribe the soldiers to say that Jesus' disciples stole his body while they were sleeping? How has the bribe and the soldiers' lies affected how people respond to Jesus since that time?

2. As people like Mary Magdalene, Cleopas, and Thomas came face to face with the risen Jesus, they had all sorts of emotions including fear, joy, and amazement. How would you have felt if you had talked with Jesus, or put your fingers in his wounds?

3. Given the biblical account as well as the historical evidence of Jesus' life, death, and resurrection, people have argued that "Jesus was either a liar, a lunatic, or the Lord of all." Based on what you have read and experienced, which do you think he is? Are there other options that could explain Jesus' identity? What does your answer mean for your life?

_____

_____

_____

_____

_____

_____

Chapter 21 More to Come *(p. 169)*

Reflect

Jesus instructed his followers to go and make disciples of all nations. He promised, "Anyone who believes and is baptized will be saved."

Jesus asked Peter three times, "Do you love me." He wants us to love him more than anything else.

Jesus proved he was alive in many ways. He appeared several times, and in different places. He taught his disciples more about the kingdom of God.

Jesus promised his disciples that they will be baptized with the Holy Spirit to have the power to be his witnesses.

The angels asked the disciples why they were standing there looking at the sky. Jesus will return!

Think

- Now, at the end of the story of Jesus, what do you believe about him and why?
- Jesus is with us now through his Spirit in us. When do you experience his presence in your life?
- Have you asked for the power of the Holy Spirit to be Jesus' witness?
- Believing in Jesus involves not just looking to heaven, but also bringing others to know Jesus. Where do you see the Holy Spirit leading you in this mission?

Pray

Talk to God in prayer about this reading. In your own words, ask God to show you what it means for your life.

Apply

Look for the phrase in the reading that most catches your attention. Underline or highlight it. Reflect on how it applies to you.

Act

What concrete action will you take to apply your prayer and reflection in your daily life?

Discuss

1. Just prior to Jesus' death, Peter denied Jesus three times and Jesus later asked Peter three times if he loved him. What point do you think Jesus was trying to make by asking Peter this question three times? How do you think Peter felt after this encounter with the risen Jesus?

2. Jesus promised that the Holy Spirit would empower his followers to be witnesses in Jerusalem (their city), Judea (their country), Samaria (their neighboring region), and in all the world. This promise holds true for his followers today. How might Jesus want you to spread the message of Jesus with the people closest to you, with people you meet, and throughout your world?

3. The last sentences in this chapter summarize the hope that the story of Jesus brings to us—that what is written will help you "believe that Jesus is the Messiah, the Son of God, and that by believing, you may have life in his name." Do you believe that Jesus is the Son of God? If not, what questions about Jesus still linger for you? If you do believe, how can you experience more of the life that comes from belonging to Jesus?

GUIDE TO PEOPLE AND TERMS

ABRAHAM lived about 4,000 years ago. He is the ancestor of both the Jewish and Arab people. Three of the world's major religions—Judaism, Islam, and Christianity—come from his descendants. You can learn more about Abraham in the Old Testament of the Bible (Genesis 12–25).

ANGELS are spiritual beings who serve God. The name comes from the Greek word for messenger.

APOSTLE is a special messenger or representative. The 12 disciples of Jesus, and other leaders of the early church, were called apostles.

BAPTISM is a ritual cleansing with water. Baptism is performed by sprinkling, pouring, or immersion according to church traditions.

CRUCIFIXION is a slow and painful death the Romans used to execute rebels. A person was nailed to a wooden cross with heavy iron nails through the wrists and heel bones. The victim was forced to push down on the nails to be able to breathe. The legs were sometimes broken to make the victim suffocate sooner.

DANIEL was a prophet who lived during the Jewish captivity in Babylon in the sixth century BC. He became famous for his skill in interpreting dreams and visions.

DAVID was a shepherd boy who became a great Jewish king about 3,000 years ago. He became famous for killing the giant Goliath (1 Samuel 17). Prophets said that the Messiah would come from the royal family line of David. Both of Jesus' parents descended from King David, but Jesus also claimed to be God's son.

DEMONS are generally regarded as some form of evil, supernatural spirits. In Jesus' time, demons were believed to be responsible for many illnesses. Jesus cast out demons and healed diseases. He spoke to demons directly; sometimes they spoke back.

DESTRUCTION OF THE TEMPLE happened as Jesus predicted. About forty years after his death, a revolt of the Jews against Roman rule ended with the Romans demolishing the temple and dispersing the Jewish people. For 2,000 years, the Jews did not have a national homeland again until the country of Israel was established in 1948.

DISCIPLE means a learner or follower. Jesus chose 12 of his many followers to be his close group of disciples. Some of these 12, like Simon (also called Peter) or Matthew (also called Levi) have more than one name in the Gospels.

DIVORCE of a wife by her husband was allowed by some of the religious leaders for any reason. However, a wife was not permitted to divorce her husband, even if he was unfaithful to her. Women had few rights and were treated like property, but Jesus treated them with respect. He preached about the spiritual significance of a man and woman joining in marriage.

ELIJAH was an important Jewish prophet who lived about 900 years before Jesus. Many Jewish people believed that Elijah would return to prepare the way for the Messiah. Jesus recalled how Elijah miraculously produced food for a starving widow and brought her son back to life (1 Kings 17:8-24).

ELISHA was Elijah's successor. Jesus told of how Elisha healed Naaman, the commander of a foreign army, from a skin disease (2 Kings 5:1-27).

FAMILY ANCESTORS OF JESUS are listed in the Gospels of Matthew (1:1-17) and Luke (3:23-38). Matthew recorded the family of Jesus through his legal father Joseph. Many Bible scholars think that

Luke recorded the family line of Jesus through his mother Mary—by custom, the name of her husband, Joseph, replaced her name in the family line.

FEAST OF SHELTERS celebrates the end of harvest. During this feast, people lived in shelters made of branches to remind them of the shelters used by their ancestors as they traveled the desert with Moses.

FOOD LAWS were based on the animals, fish, and birds prohibited in the Law of Moses (Leviticus 11:1-47; Deuteronomy 14:1-21). The Jewish people had strict rules about what food was considered to be clean, or *kosher* (a Hebrew word meaning "proper").

GENTILE is the term for a person who is not Jewish.

GOD'S NAME was claimed by Jesus. The religious leaders became angry when Jesus said "I Am" because this referred to the holy name God used when he spoke to Moses from a burning bush (Exodus 3:1-15). The Hebrew name is translated as "Yahweh" or "Jehovah" in English.

HANUKKAH (Festival of the Dedication of the Temple) celebrates the re-dedication of the temple during the second century BC after the Jewish people rebelled against a Greek king who defiled the temple.

HEROD became known as Herod the Great because of his grand building projects, including rebuilding the temple in Jerusalem. The Romans appointed him as the king of the Jews in 37 BC, and he ruled for thirty-two years. After he died, his son Herod Antipas ruled the region of Galilee where Jesus lived.

HOSANNA comes from a Hebrew expression meaning "save us." The people of Israel used this expression to appeal to their kings for help. It later became an exclamation of praise and honor to God. The people shouted this blessing to Jesus.

ISAIAH was a major Jewish prophet who lived when the Assyrians captured the ten northern tribes of Israel in 721 BC. Tradition says that he was sawed in half for speaking out against evil.

ISRAEL was the name God gave to Jacob—the son of Isaac and grandson of Abraham (Genesis 32:28). The 12 tribes of the nation of Israel were named after and descended from Jacob's sons.

JEREMIAH was a major Jewish prophet who lived when the Babylonians destroyed Jerusalem and exiled the Jewish people in 586 BC. He tried to persuade the Jewish people to repent so God would not punish them for their sins.

JESUS comes from the Greek translation of the name Joshua. It means "the Lord saves."

JOHN THE BAPTIST baptized people in the Jordan River as a sign that they had turned away from sin and received God's forgiveness. He told the people who had been baptized to change their behavior.

JOHN the disciple sometimes referred to himself in his Gospel as "the disciple Jesus loved." He also identified himself both as an eyewitness and one who wrote these things down (John 21:23-25).

JONAH was a prophet who tried to run away from God. Sailors threw him over the side of a ship during a wild storm, and he was swallowed by a huge fish sent by God. After three days, the fish spat him up alive onto dry land (Jonah 1–2).

LAKE GALILEE is an inland lake in northern Israel, where for a time Jesus lived nearby. In the Gospels, it is also called the Sea of Galilee, Lake Tiberias, or Lake Gennesaret. The lake is known for sudden storms with violent winds.

LAW OF MOSES (the Law) comprises the first five books of the Bible. It is also known as the Jewish Torah. The Law gave instructions about how to obey God and respect other people. Tradition says Moses wrote these books.

LEVITES were assistants to the temple priests. The priests were from the family line of Aaron, who was Moses' brother and the first high priest of Israel.

LOT was a nephew of Abraham who lived in the evil city of Sodom. Lot and his family fled when God destroyed this city, but Lot's wife hesitated and was turned into a pillar of salt (Genesis 19:15-29).

MANGER is a feeding box for animals. A stable, cave, or the bottom part of a house were used to shelter farm animals. So Jesus may have been born among the animals.

MANNA was the food God provided to the people of Israel when they wandered in the desert for forty years. Each night white flakes of food fell from the sky (Exodus 16:1-36). Many people of Jesus' time believed that God would again provide manna when the Messiah arrived.

MESSIAH is a Hebrew term that means "the anointed." The title "Christ" comes from the Greek translation of the term. At the time of Jesus' death, the Jewish people had been ruled by the Romans for about 100 years. They were waiting for a Messiah who would come to rule God's kingdom. Many hoped Jesus would free them from Roman occupation. Instead, Jesus preached about the reign of God in the hearts and lives of his followers.

MONEY CHANGERS provided the temple currency. Money changers and animal merchants set up their stalls in the area intended for Gentile worshipers. The temple authorities shared in the profits at the people's expense.

MOSES was a great leader who led the people of Israel out from slavery in Egypt about 3,500 years ago. The people complained as he led them through the desert, so God sent poisonous snakes to punish them. When they asked Moses to help them, God told him to make a bronze snake and lift it up on a pole. The people survived if they looked at it when they were bitten (Numbers 21:6-9). Jesus said he also would be lifted up (on a cross) to save people. Today, the symbol of a snake on a pole is used by many medical organizations.

NOAH built an ark to save his family and animals from a great flood. God brought this flood to punish humans because they had become so evil (Genesis 6–8).

PASSOVER FEAST is a Jewish festival that celebrates the escape of Israel from slavery in Egypt. God "passed over" the people's homes, sparing them, whereas the eldest son of every Egyptian family died (Exodus 11–12).

PETER was the name Jesus gave to his disciple Simon. The name means "a rock" in the Aramaic language that Jesus spoke. The Gospels refer to him by either name or sometimes by both.

PHARISEES were one of the main groups of Jewish religious leaders in the time of Jesus. The Pharisees were experts in the Law and the messages of the prophets.

PILATE was appointed by Rome to be the governor of Judea and Samaria in AD 26. Pilate had to put down several revolts by the Jewish people while he was the governor.

PROPHETS delivered messages from God to the people. These messages were often about future events. Jesus quoted the prophets and said that he had come to fulfill their message. You can find the Old Testament references for these quotations in many Bibles.

QUEEN OF THE SOUTH came from the region that is now Yemen to visit King Solomon. Also known as Queen Sheba, she praised God when she saw how much he had blessed Solomon (1 Kings 10:1-13).

RITUAL WASHING involved washing hands or other parts of the body in a certain way (also called "ablution"). The Pharisees taught people to perform the ritual to purify themselves. Devout Jews performed a ritual washing seven times a day.

SABBATH is a holy day set aside by God to be a day of rest (Exodus 20:8-11). The Pharisees made up many extra laws for the Sabbath day, including prohibiting carrying loads, picking wheat, or helping the sick. Jews observe the Sabbath from sundown on Friday until sundown on Saturday. Christians began to observe the Sabbath on the first day of the week—the day of Jesus' resurrection.

SACRIFICE was a ritual way for people to be forgiven for their sins. The priests offered several sacrifices every day in the temple in Jerusalem. The sacrifices stopped when the Romans destroyed the temple in AD 70.

SADDUCEES were the upper class of the priests and one of the factions of Jewish leaders. They accepted only the Law of Moses and did not believe in resurrection of the dead.

SAMARITANS were a mixed race of people descended from the Jews and foreigners that the Assyrians resettled in Northern Israel. The Samaritans and Jewish people generally despised each other. It was very unusual for a Jewish man even to talk to a Samaritan woman. But Jesus treated the Samaritan woman he met at a well with respect and kindness.

SANHEDRIN was the Jewish council of elders that acted as Israel's high court.

SATAN is the name of the devil—the leader of spiritual forces of evil. He is also called Beelzebul in the Gospels.

SHEPHERDS kept sheep at night in a cave or pen made of stones and branches to protect them from thieves or wild animals. The shepherd usually slept at the entrance to guard his flock. The prophet Ezekiel described the Messiah as the shepherd of people.

SODOM AND GOMORRAH were ancient cities that were known for the wickedness of their people. God destroyed these cities by fire as a punishment (Genesis 19:24-25).

SOLOMON was the son of King David. He was famous for his wisdom and wealth.

SON OF MAN is the title that Jesus often used for himself. It came from a vision of the Messiah described by the Jewish prophet Daniel. He saw God give the Son of Man supreme authority and an everlasting kingdom (Daniel 7:13-14).

TAX COLLECTORS were Jews working for the Roman authorities. They were despised as traitors who enriched themselves at the expense of their own people. Often they stole by collecting more than the taxes due.

TEMPLE CURTAIN covered the entrance to the Most Holy Place, which was the inner sanctuary where God appeared to the High Priest. The High Priest could go beyond the curtain only once a year to seek forgiveness for the people's sins. The curtain was torn open when Jesus died on the cross.

TEN COMMANDMENTS were laws given by God to Moses (Exodus 20; Deuteronomy 5). Jesus quoted from the Ten Commandments and explained their true meaning. He talked about the importance of our attitudes as well as our actions.

THEOPHILUS may have been a Roman or a Greek official. Luke dedicated his Gospel to Theophilus, whose name means "one who loves God."

TIBERIUS was the Roman emperor at the time of Jesus. He lived from AD 14 to 37.

TYRE AND SIDON were two ancient cities that God punished because of their people's sin (Ezekiel 28).

WHIPPING or scourging of prisoners by the Romans could be fatal. The whip was made of several strips of leather with pieces of sharp bone and metal attached that tore off pieces of flesh.

WORD is special term for God. John in his Gospel identified Jesus as the Word that existed in the beginning.

PLACES IN THE STORY

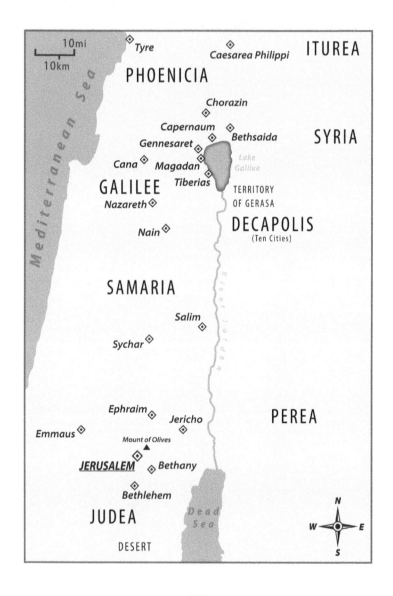

GOSPEL REFERENCES AND INDEX

	MATTHEW	MARK	LUKE	JOHN	Page
Chapter 7					
Jesus heals the commander's servant	8:5-13		7:1-10		45
Jesus raises a widow's son from the dead			7:11-17		46
Jesus talks about John the Baptist	11:1-19		7:18-35		46
Jesus promises rest for the weary	11: 25-30				48
Many women support Jesus			8:1-3		48
Jesus accused of using evil powers	12:22-37	3:22-30	11:14-28		48
Jesus asks for a sign from God	12:38-45		11:29-32		49
Jesus talks about his true family	12:46-50	3:31-35	8:19-21		49
Jesus tells a story about seed and soils	13:1-23	4:1-25	8:4-18		50
Jesus tells stories about God's kingdom	13:24-51	4:26-34	13:18-21		51
Chapter 8					
Jesus calms a storm	8:23-27	4:35-41	8:22-25		55
Jesus delivers a man from demons	8:28-34	5:1-20	8:26-39		55
A sick woman touches Jesus' clothes	9:20-22	5:25-34	8:43-48		57
Jesus brings a girl back to life	9:18-26	5:21-43	8:40-56		57
Jesus' own town rejects him	13:53-58	6:1-6		4:44	58
Jesus sends out his disciples	10:5-16	6:7-13	9:1-6		59
Jesus warns of persecution	10:17-33		12:2-12		59
Jesus warns of family strife	10:34-42		12:49-53		60
Herod kills John the Baptist	14:1-12	6:14-29	9:7-9		61
Chapter 9					
Jesus feeds 5000 people	14:13-21	6:30-44	9:10-17	6:1-15	63
Jesus walks on the lake	14:22-36	6:45-56		6:16-21	64
Jesus is "the bread of life"				6:22-71	66
Jesus talks about being "unclean"	15:1-20	7:1-23			68

	MATTHEW	MARK	LUKE	JOHN	Page
Jesus warns about sin and death			13:1-9		91
Jesus heals a woman on the Sabbath			13:10-17		91
Jesus heals a blind man on the Sabbath				9:1-41	92
Jesus says he is "the good shepherd"				10:1-18	94
Jesus is accused of being crazy		3:20-21		10:19-21	95
Jesus says he is God's son				10:22-42	96
Chapter 13					
Jesus talks about the narrow way	8:11-12		13:22-30		97
Jesus grieves over Jerusalem	23:37-39		13:31-35		98
Jesus heals a man with a swollen body			14:1-6		98
Jesus tells stories about feasts	22:1-14		14:7-24		98
Jesus talks about the cost of following him			14:25-35		100
Jesus tells a story of a prodigal son			15:11-32		101
Jesus tells a story about a clever manager			16:1-15		102
Jesus tells a story about a beggar and the rich man			16:19-31		103
Jesus' friend Lazarus dies				11:1-16	104
Jesus is "the resurrection and life"				11:17-27	105
Jesus raises Lazarus from the dead				11:28-44	106
Jewish leaders plan to kill Jesus				11:45-54	107
Chapter 14					
Jesus heals ten men with skin diseases			17:11-19		109
Jesus talks about his kingdom			17:20-37		109
Jesus tells stories about prayer			18:1-14		110
Jesus talks about divorce	19:1-12	10:1-12	16:16-18		112

	MATTHEW	MARK	LUKE	JOHN	Page
Jesus meets a rich young man	19:16-30	10:17-31	18:18-30		112
Jesus tells a story about vineyard workers	20:1-16				113
Jesus predicts his death	20:17-19	10:32-34	18:31-34		114
James and John ask for favor	20:20-28	10:35-45			114
Jesus gives sight to Bartimaeus	20:29-34	10:46-52	18:35-43		115
Jesus meets Zacchaeus			19:1-10		116
Jesus tells a story about ten servants	25:14-30		19:11-27		116
Jesus is welcomed as king	21:1-9	11:1-10	19:28-40	12:12-19	117
Chapter 15					
Jesus enters Jerusalem	21:10-11	11:11	19:41-44		119
Jesus clears the temple	21:12-13	11:15-17	19:45-46	2:12-23	120
Jesus meets Greeks				12:20-36	120
Jewish leaders reject Jesus	21:14-16	11:18	19:47-48	12:37-50	121
Jesus dries up a fig tree	21:17-22	11:12-26			122
Leaders question Jesus' authority	21:23-27	11:27-33	20:1-8		122
Jesus tells stories about vineyards	21:28-46	12:1-12	20:9-19		123
Jesus talks about taxes	22:15-22	12:13-17	20:20-26		124
Jesus talks about resurrection	22:23-33	12:18-27	20:27-40		125
Jesus states the first commandment	22:34-40	12:28-34			125
Jesus questions religious leaders	22:41-46	12:35-37	20:41-44		126
Jesus condemns religious leaders	23:1-36	12:38-40	11:37-54 20:45-47		126
Chapter 16					
A poor widow makes an offering		12:41-44	21:1-4		129
Jesus predicts the destruction of the temple	24:1-2	13:1-2	21:5-6		129
Jesus talks about signs of the end of the world	24:3-22	13:3-20	21:7-26		130
Jesus talks about his future return	24:23-35	13:21-32	21:27-38		131

	MATTHEW	MARK	LUKE	JOHN	Page
Jesus explains how to be ready for his return	24:36-51	13:33-37	12:35-48		131
Jesus tells a story about bridesmaids	25:1-13				132
Jesus discusses the final judgment of everyone	25:31-46				133
A woman pours perfume on Jesus	26:6-13	14:3-9	7:36-50	12:1-11	134
Chapter 17					
Judas agrees to betray Jesus	26:1-16	14:10-11	22:1-6		137
Disciples prepare the Passover meal	26:17-19	14:12-16	22:7-13		137
Jesus washes his disciples' feet				13:1-17	138
Jesus shares the last supper	26:20-30	14:17-26	22:14-30	13:18-32	139
Jesus predicts Peter's denial	26:31-35	14:27-31	22:31-38	13:33-38	140
Jesus is the "way, truth, and life"				14:1-14	141
Jesus promises to send the Holy Spirit				14:15-31	142
Jesus commands us to love each other				15:1-17	143
Jesus talks about persecution				15:18-16:4	143
Jesus is returning to the Father				16:5-33	144
Jesus prays for his followers				17:1-26	146
Jesus sweats blood in Gethsemane	26:36-46	14:32-42	22:39-46	18:1-2	148
Jesus is betrayed and arrested	26:47-56	14:43-52	22:47-54	18:3-12	148
Chapter 18					
Jesus is tried by the Jewish council	26:57-66	14:53-64	22:54	18:13-24	151
Guards beat and abuse Jesus	26:67-68	14:65	22:63-65		152
Peter denies knowing Jesus	26:69-75	14:66-72	22:55-62	18:15-27	152
Jesus is sentenced to die	27:1-2	15:1	22:66-71		152
Judas Iscariot hangs himself	27:3-10				152
Jesus is tried by Pilate	27:11-14	15:2-5	23:1-6	18:28-38	153

*Two references from Acts are included because Luke continues the story in the book of Acts.

LETTERS FROM CHURCH LEADERS

The Pope's letter and blessing for *God with Us.*

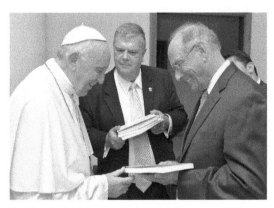

Pope Francis and editors reviewing *God with Us.*

Oficina del Cardenal

Sisters and brothers:

It is an immense joy to present the book *God with Us*. It was produced in response to Point 29 of the Document of Aparecida:

> We want the joy that we have received in the encounter with Jesus Christ, whom we recognize as Son of God incarnate and redeemer, to reach all men and women wounded by adversities; we want the good news of the Kingdom of God, of Jesus Christ victorious over sin and death, to reach all who lie along the roadside, asking for alms and compassion (cf. Luke 10: 29-37; 18:25-43). The disciple's joy serves as remedy for a world fearful of the future and overwhelmed by violence and hatred. The disciple's joy is not a feeling of selfish well-being, but a certainty that springs from faith, that soothes the heart and provides the ability to proclaim the good news of God's love. Knowing Jesus is the best gift that any person can receive; that we have encountered him is the best thing that has happened in our lives and making him known by our word and deeds is our joy.

It is always a joy to be able to announce Jesus Christ, especially through the texts of the Gospels, which are presented here in chronological order. At the end of each chapter, we have included *Lectio Divina* exercises to help those who wish to follow Jesus, and as his disciples reflect on their vocation.

We hope that it will serve everyone, especially young people who seek to follow Christ, so that by having an overview of the life of Jesus they can meditate on their vocation and on the way of living as witnesses of the Risen One; with coherent answers from the Gospels for our world today, in the third Christian millennium.

+ Oscar Andrés Cardenal Rodríguez Maradiaga, S.D.B
Archbishop of Tegucigalpa, Honduras,
Coordinator of the Council of Cardinals
Honorary President of Ramón Pané Foundation

OFFICE OF THE ARCHBISHOP

Dear Brothers and Sisters in Christ,

In the Gospel of John, we hear the story of some people who came to the Apostle Philip, and they asked him, "We wish to see Jesus!"

We all need to see Jesus. Because only when we come to meet Jesus and know his love, does our life truly begin. Only Jesus can show us the face of the Father.

Our encounter with Jesus begins in the pages of the Gospels. In these pages, we meet the Son of the living God. And by listening to his words and reflecting on his example, we come to know that God is with us.

Pope Francis says we should all carry a small copy of the Gospels that can fit in our pockets, and we should pull it out and read it whenever we can. We should read a passage every day from the Gospel, the Pope tells us, because it is the only way we can get to know Jesus.

God with Us is a unique book that can help us in our search to see Jesus and to know him. This book draws from the stories of the four Gospels and arranges them to form a single, unified narrative, a kind of biography, in which we encounter Jesus Christ, who is Emmanuel, God with us.

This book also provides questions for reflection and meditation that invite us to read this story prayerfully and personally, in the spirit of the ancient technique of *Lectio Divina* or sacred reading.

If prayer is conversation, then we need to listen to God as much as we talk to him. "When you read the Bible, God speaks to you," St. Augustine said. "When you pray, you speak to God." We should never read the life of Jesus as students gathering information to prepare for a test. Instead, we should read as friends who want to know everything we can about the One we love—the details of his life; what he is saying and thinking; how he responds to different situations in his life; his attitudes and feelings.

Reading the daily Gospel with prayer, our lives become a journey we are making with Jesus, a pilgrimage of the heart. The more we pray with the Gospels, the more we will have "the mind of Christ"—his thoughts and feelings, seeing reality through his eyes. The more we pray with the Gospels, the more we will feel Christ's call to change the world—to shape society and history according to God's loving plan.

So, I pray that *God with Us* will help you to learn to love spending time with Jesus in the reading of sacred Scripture!

There is beautiful description of how Blessed Virgin Mary reflected on what she experienced: "But Mary kept all these things, pondering them in her heart" [Luke 2:19, RSV]. This is a lesson for us. We need to keep Jesus close to our heart—his words, his actions, the scenes from his life. We need to ponder them and pray about them. Just like Mary did.

May our Blessed Mother Mary accompany all of us as we come to the pages of the Gospels, seeking to see Jesus.

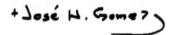

Most Reverend Jose H. Gomez
Archbishop of Los Angeles
President of the United States Conference of Catholic Bishops.

ARCHDIOCESE OF MIAMI
Office of the Archbishop

Dearest Brothers and Sisters:

The mission and identity of the church is to evangelize. That is, bring the good news of the Gospel of our Lord Jesus Christ to all peoples without distinction. When we get started in the project of the Church we come closer to holiness. The Saints are those who assume the life of Christ as their own. Therefore, it is necessary that we truly get to know the life of Christ in order to follow Him. With this purpose, in his recent Apostolic Exhortation, Pope Francis lets us know the following:

> 19. A Christian cannot think of his or her mission on earth without seeing it as a path of holiness, for "this is the will of God, your sanctification" (1 Thessalonians 4:3, RSV). Each saint is a mission, planned by the Father to reflect and embody, at a specific moment in history, a certain aspect of the Gospel.

> 20. That mission has its fullest meaning in Christ and can only be understood through him. At its core, holiness is experiencing, in union with Christ, the mysteries of his life. It consists in uniting ourselves to the Lord's death and resurrection in a unique and personal way, constantly dying and rising anew with him. But it can also entail reproducing in our own lives various aspects of Jesus' earthly life: his hidden life, his life in community, his closeness to the outcast, his poverty, and other ways in which he showed his self-sacrificing love. The contemplation of these mysteries, as Saint Ignatius of Loyola pointed out, leads us to incarnate them in our choices and attitudes. Because "everything in Jesus' life was a sign of his mystery", "Christ's whole life is a revelation of the Father", "Christ's whole life is a mystery of redemption", "Christ's whole life is a mystery of recapitulation". "Christ enables us to live in him all that he himself lived, and he lives it in us". (*Gaudete et Exsultate* 19–20)

I have the pleasure of presenting this work called *God with Us*, which was put together with great care by Fundación Ramón Pané, to help its readers know the life of Jesus as written directly by Matthew, Mark, Luke, and John. The texts were ordered in a harmonious and chronological format to help the readers to truly "follow of Christ," because in following Christ we can achieve holiness. At the end of each chapter some questions were added using the method of *Lectio Divina* to help the reader reflect along this path of holiness.

Pope Francis, who dedicated a "Chirograph," or excerpt in his own handwriting, for this book invites us to be disciples as well as missionaries in this work. In *Gaudete et Exsultate* he also tells us:

> "Each in his or her own way" the Council says. We should not grow discouraged before examples of holiness that appear unattainable. There are some testimonies that may prove helpful and inspiring, but that we are not meant to copy, for that could even lead us astray from the one specific path that the Lord has in mind for us. The important thing is that each believer discerns his or her own path, that they bring out the very best of themselves, the most personal gifts that God has placed in their hearts (cf. 1 Corinthians 12:7), rather than hopelessly trying to imitate something not meant for them. We are all called to be witnesses, but there are many actual ways of bearing witness. (*Gaudete et Exsultate* 11).

This work also can be used as an evangelizing tool, especially by those that are first getting to know Christ. We wish it to be used especially by young people that have taken on the mission of evangelizing their peers within their social circles.

I too want to impart my blessing to those who read the Gospel and have a desire to become announcers of the Good News.

Archbishop Thomas Wenski
Archbishop of Miami

Fundación
Ramón Pané

My life is permanent travel. God has blessed me with knowing many places in the world, especially as a missionary and evangelizer. But the greatest benefit is not all the many landscapes, which undoubtedly speak of the Creator, it is the people. Meeting people from different cultures, ages, social situations, and very different ways of thinking helps me grow in this process called the Christian life.

As a disciple and missionary evangelist, I seriously wonder if we are doing as Jesus asked: Go to all peoples everywhere and make them my disciples (Matthew 28:19). The emphasis is on the imperative "go" and I ask myself: What have we done as disciples and missionaries with this commandment? Maybe there is enthusiasm in many places, but I still ask myself: Am I effective in reaching beyond those who participate in our church groups? The *Lectio Divina* exercises provided for each chapter of this book aim to reinforce our Christian vocation as disciples who become missionaries.

The Ramon Pane Foundation is very proud to put in your hands this tool that will be useful for those who only know Jesus from what others say but have not read the Gospels themselves. It is the complete story from the Gospels told chronologically. To facilitate reading, the chapter and verse numbers were eliminated; but the reference for each scripture selection is included for anyone interested in looking for it in the Bible.

We encourage you to become a disciple transformed into a missionary who distributes this simple tool to help many come to know Jesus from the original writings of the New Testament presented in a fresh, new, and concise way.

Courage in your walk!

Bro. Ricardo Grzona, FRP
Director General
Fraternity of Ramón Pané

Young friends, don't wait until tomorrow to contribute your energy,
your audacity, and your creativity to changing our world.
Pope Francis

Milton Keynes UK
Ingram Content Group UK Ltd.
UKHW020708290823
427678UK00015B/607